WRITING A RESEARCH PAPER

FIFTH EDITION

JONATHA CEELY
HELEN W. DUNN
MARY TYLER KNOWLES
JUDITH ROBBINS

WAYSIDE PUBLISHING

129 Commonwealth Ave
Concord MA 01742
(888) 302-2519

To our Expository Writing students, past, present, and future.

Acknowledgment / Figure Legend

Picture page 103: From UNVEILING THE EDGE OF TIME: BLACK HOLES, WHITE HOLES, WORMHOLES by John Gribbin. Copyright © 1992 by John Gribbin and Mary Gribbin. Reprinted by permission of Harmony Books, a division of Crown Publishers, Inc.

Pictures pages 105 and 106: From BLACK HOLES by Clifford A. Pickover, Copyright © 1996 by Clifford A. Pickover. Reprinted by permission of John Wiley & Sons, Inc.

Writing a Research Paper, Fifth Edition

ISBN 1-877653-66-7

Contents

Preface

Writing a research paper is not a single action but a series of interlocked steps, a process. Throughout this brief manual it has been our aim to define this process and to give reasons for including each step. The students who use this manual thoughtfully, understanding and mastering each stage of the paper-writing process, should acquire a tool they can employ in any discipline that requires written work. It is our hope that students will discover that a system, a structure, can liberate rather than restrict, for we believe that mastering the means of communication is but a step toward a more important goal—the free exchange of ideas.

The idea for this manual has been developed over several years and through four editions. As we launch this fifth edition, we continue to be grateful to the Language Arts Summer Workshop, Lexington Public Schools, Lexington, Massachusetts, whose work helped us as we began to teach our own Expository Writing course. We also thank Arlene Rubin, who indefatigably provided the material on the use of the library that anchored the first editions of this manual. Since then, we and our students have benefited immeasurably from the expert teaching of Ellen Berne on the use and evaluation of Internet sources and electronic indexes. In addition we thank Jennett Vosburgh, whose thoughtful comments have enabled us to navigate the complexities of the ever-evolving World Wide Web with greater confidence; Eric Wirth of the Modern Language Association, who provided invaluable advice on bibliographic form; and Jennifer Skeele, Albert Steg, and Helen Young, master teachers, whose editing suggestions have made this a stronger work. Finally, we are grateful to the Winsor School for providing the setting in which we could develop and test our material, and to all of our students for their thoughtful and courteous responses to the strengths and weaknesses of this material as it has developed over the past twenty-one years.

THE
RESEARCH
PROCESS

I
Selecting a Worthwhile Subject

A. THE CHOICE OF TOPIC

It is not necessary to choose for your research paper a topic on which you are already well informed; rather, choose an area about which you are curious and wish to know more. When a possible subject occurs to you, investigate the resources of the libraries that are available to you and begin a tentative bibliography. (See III A.) This activity serves three purposes. First, it reveals whether experts have already treated your topic so thoroughly that you would be merely repeating their research. Second, it reveals whether the topic is so limited or so esoteric that there is insufficient material on it. Third, it reveals whether the material is merely popular and superficial.

B. THE FACTUAL RESEARCH PAPER

The topic chosen and the kind of material available on it will tend to determine whether the final paper is a factual or problem-centered paper. If, for example, you wish to write about American Indian craft techniques or the life cycle of a turtle, you will probably find that your final paper is essentially descriptive in its presentation of material. Of course, you will need to develop a clear thesis that limits and focuses your research, but you will rely on the assertions of experts rather than on your own analysis of primary sources as you support that thesis. Thus, the factual paper brings together reliable information and the ideas of recognized experts in order to define and describe an area of knowledge. (See Appendixes A and B for examples of factual research papers.)

C. THE PROBLEM-CENTERED RESEARCH PAPER

A problem-centered paper seeks a solution to a problem. The problem-centered paper has these characteristics: recognizing a problem, stating an hypothesis, analyzing it, presenting data from a variety of sources, and coming to a conclusion inferred from the data presented. Based on investigation and the weighing of valid research materials, this conclusion should be the major emphasis of the paper and should be the writer's own. Thus, the problem-centered paper differs from the factual paper even though both require substantial research, and both may seek answers to a question. The problem-centered paper has a conclusion which may involve any of the following: assessment, analysis, evaluation, or interpretation. Whereas the factual paper is largely an exercise in compiling and reporting facts, the problem-centered paper goes one step further by making valid inferences or presenting conclusions clearly drawn from the data presented. See Appendix C for an example of a problem-centered paper written by a student who uses particularly sophisticated vocabulary and syntax to express her ideas.

D. NEED FOR AN EARLY AND CLEAR STATEMENT OF TOPIC

Because you will not be able to handle the research

process efficiently if your topic is too broad, limit and clearly state the topic as a phrase or sentence as soon as possible. The narrowing process might proceed in this way:

> General area of interest: Significant 20th Century American Women
> General topic: Eleanor Roosevelt
> Limited topic: How Eleanor Roosevelt changed from a dependent to an independent woman

In exploring your general area of interest, you might read widely in several anthologies, but your research for this paper will begin with a biography of Eleanor Roosevelt and then be further limited to particular periods or incidents in her life.

The process of narrowing the topic of a factual paper is similar:

> General area of interest: Ecology
> General topic: The Salt Marsh
> Limited topic: How the balanced ecosystem of the salt marsh is vulnerable to pollution

If the limited topic is developed primarily by the use of description, it will be a factual paper. Notice, however, that the line between the factual and the problem-centered paper can be a very fine one. The treatment you choose for your topic will depend on the kind of material your research reveals and the approach to it that you prefer. What remains essential is that the broad, fuzzy general topic be narrowed to a clearly defined, concisely stated limited topic. Do not hesitate as your research progresses to shift the emphasis or refine the wording of your limited topic; do be sure that at all times the scope of your research and the statement of limited topic are precisely and logically linked.

II
Finding Sources

Begin your research by looking up your general topic in library catalogs, periodical and newspaper indexes, and the major encyclopedias. Look for varied, substantial, and reliable sources, including books, periodical articles, and material found by Internet search engines. Depending on your topic, you might also use newspaper articles, pictures, films, television programs, and telephone, e-mail, or face-to-face interviews. If catalogs and indexes do not show books or articles on your topic, go back to your general area of interest. For example, if you find nothing under the heading "Salt Marsh," go back to the general heading of "Ecology." Be flexible and imaginative in thinking of catalog and Internet search headings under which material of interest to you might be filed.

A. LIBRARY CATALOGS

Although it may be in one of several forms (cards, books, microfilm, electronic), the main function of the library catalog is to indicate which specific books the library has on your topic.

A library catalog lists every book in the library (and sometimes in a network of cooperating libraries) by author, title, and general subject in either a card index, a book, or a computer program. Occasionally microfilm catalogs use film to list every book in a library by author, title, and general subject; each film entry is read by looking at the screen of a film reader. The call number will be at the bottom of each film entry. Computer (or online) catalogs provide information by asking the researcher either to choose topics from a menu format or to type the name of an author, a book title, or a general subject heading. The citations for relevant books or articles will then appear on the computer screen. There is no single format for such catalogs; however, they tend to be easy to use because they present the researcher with instructions to follow.

No matter which system a library uses, each book will have an identifying call number to indicate where it is located on the library shelves.

Once you have found citations for your topic, jot down the call numbers for promising books and browse in the section(s) of the library where the books are shelved. Much valuable information can be located in this way.

B. ENCYCLOPEDIAS

You may wish to begin your research by consulting an encyclopedia, for a well-edited encyclopedia is an excellent tool for research. First, it will let you know whether your general topic is an appropriate heading under which to find information. Second, it will give you an overview of your subject and indicate whether it is one that is worth further exploration. Use only one encyclopedia as a source. The synopsis of a subject provided by most encyclopedias is useful, but the body of your research must go beyond such a general approach.

1. *Encyclopedia Americana*—Excellent for all North American topics as well as for scientific and technical topics. Includes biographies of living people and essays on individual works of art, music, and literature. Frequently updated.
2. *The New Encyclopedia Britannica*—More scholarly, but

more difficult to use because it has two separate parts, the Micropedia (brief coverage of selected topics) and the Macropedia (coverage of topics in depth). You *must* use the index to find all the information on your topic as well as the location of information in this encyclopedia. Truly international in scope and contains more biographies than any other encyclopedia.

3. *Collier's Encyclopedia*—Easiest to understand of these three encyclopedias and the most heavily indexed. Particularly good for current economic conditions and problems; includes analysis as well as facts. Comprehensive 12,000-item bibliography in the last volume in addition to shorter bibliographies at the end of many of the articles.

4. Specialized Encyclopedias—*Encyclopedia of Bioethics, McGraw-Hill Encyclopedia of World Biography, International Encyclopedia of the Social Sciences, McGraw-Hill Encyclopedia of Science and Technology, Notable American Women,* etc.

If you are using a multi-volume encyclopedia in book form, be sure to consult the index volume in order to find all possible references to your topic and to related topics. If you are using an encyclopedia on CD-ROM, be sure to use the search function. Be aware of the helpful bibliographies which usually appear at the end of longer articles.

C. PERIODICAL INDEXES

For most current topics, articles in periodicals will be useful. To find such articles, consult general and specialized book indexes, film indexes, electronic library indexes, and, for recent information, online databases such as ProQuest Direct, Ebsco, Electric Library, and Lexis-Nexis, which are usually available through libraries or on a pay-per-use basis.

1. *Reader's Guide to Periodical Literature*—Indexes the majority of popular magazines and is the best known and most generally available. It is, however, not the best source to consult for a specialized topic.
2. *Access: The Supplementary Index to Periodicals*—Designed to complement *Reader's Guide. Access* includes only those magazines not included in the *Reader's Guide* list. It also indexes regional and city magazines.
3. *Magazine Index*—A film and electronic index to general magazines that combines the most popular titles from *Reader's Guide* and *Access*; useful for book, theater, art reviews, and current information. Updated monthly.
4. *Art Index*—Indexes art publications of all types including yearbooks and museum bulletins; also includes entries for reproductions of works of art and book reviews. (For the teaching of art, also consult *Education Index.*)
5. *Biography Index*—Indexes biographical information in books, periodicals, pamphlets, prefaces, and the *New York Times* obituaries. Includes an index to occupations and professions.
6. *Education Index*—Indexes magazines, yearbooks, and monographs. Subjects include education, learning psychology, and physical education.
7. *General Science Index*—Begun in 1978, this index provides a guide to scientific, medical, and technical periodicals and journals at a more accessible level than *Applied Science and Technology Index.*
8. *Humanities Index* (formerly *Social Sciences and Humanities Index*)—Indexes area studies, folklore, history, language and literature, performing arts, philosophy, religion and theology, journalism, motion picture reviews, and book reviews.
9. *P.A.I.S. (Public Affairs Information Service)*—Indexes publications on all subjects having to do with contem-

porary public issues and public policy. Included are eco-
nomics, history, political science, and sociology.
Publications indexed include magazines, books, government documents, and reports on public and private
organizations. Also available online.

10. *Social Sciences Index* (formerly *Social Sciences and
    Humanities Index*)—Includes anthropology, economics,
    geography, law and criminology, political science, psy-
    chology, social work and public welfare, sociology, and
    urban studies. Also includes book reviews pertaining to
    these subjects.

Some of the above indexes are published both elec-
tronically and in hard copy. Libraries may subscribe to
either form; check with the reference librarian.

D. NEWSPAPER INDEXES

For the most current approach to a topic, consult your
daily newspaper or online news databases. Access to previously published material may also be obtained from
online databases on CD-ROM or from newspaper indexes
in book form.

1. *The New York Times Index*—Gives summaries of important news, editorials and features published in the *New
   York Times*.
2. *Wall Street Journal Index*—Indexes current business
   and economic information as it appears in the *Wall
   Street Journal*.
3. Local newspaper indexes. Most city newspapers main-
   tain indexes, but public access is very limited. Libraries
   frequently have indexes for the larger newspapers and
   may also subscribe to online databases.

E. INTERNET SOURCES AND SEARCH ENGINES

To find information useful for your topic, you may wish to use an Internet search engine, an electronic retrieval system that reviews numerous public and private files available on the network of computers that form the Internet. Once you are connected to an Internet provider (a commercial subscription service such as aol.com or a public access service provided by a library or educational institution), you may choose a search engine. The type of search engine you choose will dictate your method of researching your topic.

1. Subject Heading Search Engines—These engines search a selected group of documents on the Internet according to subject headings, e.g. Science and Technology, Education, Arts and Literature. To use this type of engine, narrow a topic by steps; for example, a search on yahoo.com proceeded through the following levels: Science, Meteorology, Weather Phenomenon, El Niño and La Niña, producing thirty-two items at the final, most specific, level, including a site that provided a bibliography on the topic. Some examples of engines that search by subject heading are Yahoo, The Mining Company, Lycos AtoZ, Internet Public Library.

2. Key Word Search Engines—These engines search through all available documents on the Internet to find articles that use a word or words entered by the researcher. Such searches can produce overwhelming results. A search for El Niño, for example, could result in a list of documents and web sites that include Niño and El as separate words as well as the combination El Niño. Read directions and help links to be sure that you are using a particular engine efficiently; e.g. entering El+Niño can assure that you get only those sources that use these words together. Two examples of engines that search by key word are Alta Vista and Infoseek.

3. **Meta-Search Engines**—These "super engines" search other search engines—subject heading engines, key word search engines and other meta-search engines—to find data on a topic. For a narrow topic, a meta-search engine, such as Webcrawler, Dogpile, or Northern Light, can be a useful research tool. For example, a search for El Niño using dogpile.com brought up a list of fourteen subsidiary search engines, such as Yahoo, Thunderstone, and Magellan, listing as few as three entries (Lycos Top 5%) and as many as four thousand entries (Excite Web Search). Be aware that meta-search engines and new projects to create an all-encompassing index for the World Wide Web are constantly evolving.

In summary: explore a variety of sources. Many libraries have open-stack systems, and thus you can browse in the areas appropriate to your topic. Once you have found the call numbers for several books, examine the shelves in their area for further pertinent information. Look not only at the title of a book in your subject area but also at its table of contents and index to determine whether there will be chapters relevant to your research. In addition, you can browse on the Internet, experimenting with different ways of searching or finding links from one source to another. Because you will probably begin with a general survey of sources and you may quickly feel inundated with information, be sure to keep an accurate log of the most useful call numbers for library resources and the most promising Internet addresses.

When using any library or electronic resource center, remember that the function of a librarian or a technology consultant is to assist the public as well as to take care of the materials and facilities. ASK if you cannot find what you need or are unsure how to use any available hardware.

III
Making a Bibliography

A working bibliography is a compilation of sources which you think will be useful in researching your subject; it consists of index cards on each of which you have recorded information about *one* likely source. This information will help you keep track of your sources during the research process and will be useful later in writing the final bibliography for the finished paper.

As you consult catalogs, indexes, and Internet sources for possible material, be sure that the sources you actually include in your working bibliography are both available and pertinent to your topic. Because information on scientific subjects is continually being updated and because methods of historical and biographical research change, your bibliography should consist primarily of sources published within the last twenty-five years (check publication date); however, you should not overlook earlier definitive works in your subject area, nor should you fail to include primary sources when appropriate.

Not only must your sources be timely, but your authors must also be competent in their respective fields. There are several ways of determining reliability for both print and electronic sources:

1. Check the format of the book, article or electronic source. Does it have notes, citations to other sources, references that you can check? Does the work occur in the works cited or bibliographies of other works in the same field?
2. See what information is given on the book jacket, in the

preface, or in the introduction about the author. Note that information about authors may be given at the beginning or near the end of a journal or magazine. In the case of an Internet source, check that the author or creator of the information is identified and that credentials for the individual or group are indicated. What is the reputation of the author or organization? Use sources that are intended to teach and inform rather than those designed to persuade or sell.

3. For material from all sources, consider where the information comes from. Can you verify any of the information from your own knowledge or by comparison to other independent sources? Does the language or tone or the use of anecdotal material seem biased? [1]

BE AWARE THAT THERE MAY BE A VARIETY OF POINTS OF VIEW ON YOUR TOPIC.

A. THE FORM FOR THE BIBLIOGRAPHY ENTRY

You must be consistent in the form you use to record bibliographical information. While there are various correct ways of writing bibliography entries, the Modern Language Association (MLA) recommendations which provide guidelines for this manual are widely accepted. The bibliography entry consists of the following parts:

1. Author (or editor).
2. Title (of book or article).
3. Publication facts:
    a. for books: city, publisher(s), date

---

[1] For material in this checklist we are indebted to Ellen Berne, Director of the Virginia Wing Library, The Winsor School, Boston, Massachusetts.

  b. for encyclopedias: name, edition, and/or year
  c. for periodicals: title, volume or number for a schol-
     arly journal, date, pages
  d. for Internet and other electronic media sources:
     see C 2 in this chapter.

These divisions are separated by periods. The necessary
information will be on the title page and on the back of the
title page. If some information is not given, write n.d. (for
no data available) in the appropriate place in the entry. *Be
sure to record all data in correct bibliographic form.*

B. WRITING A BIBLIOGRAPHY CARD

Following the appropriate form in the examples below,
make a bibliography card for every useful source; be sure
to do each card completely, in ink. In a few cases, the
examples and following directives call for more information than is required for a formal bibliography entry (e.g.,
volume and page of an encyclopedia article) because you
may need to refer to this information again. The sample
bibliography entries in Section III C provide models for
the types of sources which you will encounter most frequently. If you need to record a source for which no model
is provided, consult the current edition of the *MLA
Handbook for Writers of Research Papers.*

  It is *absolutely essential* that you code each bibliography card at the upper right-hand corner. The code for each
source consists of the first letter of the author's last name
followed by the first letter of the first word of the title,
excluding *a*, *an*, and *the.* You will use these code designa-
tions on your note cards to identify the sources which you
have used in your research. Also, note in parentheses at
the lower right corner the library from which you bor-
rowed the book. Additionally, you may find it useful to
write the library call number at the lower left.

General Model

```
                        Code
Author. Title.

Place: Publisher, date.

Library          (Library)
Call Number
```

For a Complete Book

```
                          RA
Reader, John. Africa:
Biography of the Continent.
New York, NY: Alfred A.
Knopf, 1998.

(DT20.R43)  (Boston Public
                    Library)
```

For an Item in a Collection

```
                          JC
Johns, Jeremy. "Christianity
and Islam." The Oxford
Illustrated History of
Christianity. Ed. John
McManners. New York, NY:
Oxford University Press,
1990. 163-195.

(270 098M 1990)  (Newton
              Public Library)
```

For a Signed Magazine Article from an Online Subscription Service

```
                          DP
Djilas, Aleksa. "A Profile of
Slobodan Milosevic." Foreign
Affairs Summer 1993
Platinum Periodicals. UMI-
ProQuest Direct.
<http://proquest.umi.com/>
(viewed 21 Apr. 1999).

   (Winsor School Library)
```

For a Signed Encyclopedia Entry

```
                          WW
Wright, Esmond.
"Washington, George."
Collier's Encyclopedia. Vol.
23. 1987 ed. 282-289.

          (Winsor Library)
```

For a Signed Newspaper Item

```
                          KN
Kobak, Annette. "No Man a
Hero to His Sled Dogs." Rev.
of Nansen: The Explorer as
Hero by Roland Huntford.
The New York Times Book
Review 16 May 1999: 16.

                     (NYPL)
```

C. BIBLIOGRAPHY SAMPLES

The following is a series of bibliography samples, not a formal bibliography. A formal bibliography is arranged in alphabetical order by author's last name.

1. Printed Works

a. Single Works

1) *Book by one author*

Cook, Fred J. Maverick: Fifty Years of Investigative Reporting. New York: G. P. Putnam's Sons, 1984.

2) *Another book by the same author*

- - -. The Ku Klux Klan: America's Recurring Nightmare. Englewood Cliffs, NJ: J. Messner, 1980.

3) *Book by two authors*

Manley, Sean, and Susan Belcher. O, Those Extraordinary Women! Philadelphia: Chilton Book Co., 1972.

4) *Book by three or more authors*

Masterton, William L., et al. Chemical Principles. Philadelphia: Saunders College Publishing, 1985.

5) *Edited work of one author*

Lawrence, D. H. Complete Poems. Eds. Vivian de Sola Pinto and F. Warren Roberts. New York: Viking Press, 1971.

6) *Translation*

Cortazar, Julio. Around the Day in Eighty Worlds. Trans. Thomas Christensen. San Francisco: North Point Press, 1986.

7) *Corporate Author*

American Medical Association. The American Medical Association's Handbook of First Aid and Emergency Care. New York: Random House, 1980.

8) *Conference Proceedings*
Proceedings of the 1985 State Fish and Wildlife
Directors Conference. 4-6 June 1985.
Washington, DC: U.S. Department of Commerce,
National Marine Fisheries Service, 1986.
9) *Occasional report*
Mendelsohn, Everett. A Human Reconstruction of
Science. A report prepared for a conference on
women. Cambridge, MA: Radcliffe Institute, April
1972.

b. Collections
1) *Previously published work in a collection*
Fox, Paula. "News from the World." Confrontation
(Spring 1975): 78-81. Rpt. in Short Shorts: An
Anthology of the Shortest Stories. Eds. Irving
Howe and Ilana Wiener Howe. Boston: David R.
Godine, 1982. 242-247.
2) *Work in an edited collection*
Liska, George. "War and Order." Globalism and Its
Critics. Ed. William Taubman. Lexington, MA: D.
C. Heath and Co., 1973. 40-52.
3) *Edited collection from which two or more works
have been cited*
Williams, Robert H., ed. To Live and To Die: When,
Why and How. New York: Springer-Verlag, 1973.

c. Encyclopedias
1) *Signed article in an encyclopedia*
Wright, Esmond. "Washington, George." Collier's
Encyclopedia. 1987 ed.
2) *Unsigned article in an encyclopedia*
"Icarus." Encyclopedia Americana. 1989 ed.

d. Revisions and Republications
1) *Reprint or facsimile of an earlier edition*

Braddon, Mary Elizabeth. Lady Audley's Secret.
1887. New York: Dover, 1974.
2) *Reprint with new foreword, afterword or introduction*
Crane, Stephen. The Red Badge of Courage. 1895.
Afterword by Clifton Fadiman. New York:
Macmillan, 1967.
3) *Edition other than the first*
Baum, Lawrence. The Supreme Court. 3rd ed.
Washington, DC: Congressional Quarterly Press,
1989.

e. Magazines, Journals and Newspapers
1) *Signed magazine article*
Murphy, Cait. "Hong Kong: A Culture of
Emigration." The Atlantic Apr. 1991: 20-26.
2) *Unsigned magazine article*
"Presidential Commission Cites Improvements in
European Airport and Airway Safety." Aviation
Week 26 Feb. 1990: 31.
3) *Journal article*
Mendelson, Edward. "Word Processing: A Guide for
the Perplexed." Yale Review 74 (1985): 615-640.
4) *Unsigned newspaper article showing edition*
"Alaska Oil by Land & Sea." New York Times 17
July 1977, nat'l ed.: A4.

f. Government Documents
1) *Printed by Government Printing Office*
a) *Report by a government department*
United States. Bureau of Labor Statistics. A Brief
History of the American Labor Movement. 1970
ed. Washington, DC: GPO, 1970.
b) *Report of hearings*
United States. Congress. Senate. Committee on
Government Operations. Subcommittee on

Intergovernmental Relations. Committee on the
Judiciary. Subcommittees on Separation of
Powers and on Administrative Practice and
Procedure. Hearings. 93rd Congress, 1st session.
12 vols. Washington, DC: GPO, 1946.

2) *Printed by private publisher*

United States. National Advisory Commission on
Civil Disorders. Report of the National Advisory
Commission on Civil Disorders. New York Times
Edition. New York: E.P. Dutton, 1969.

g. Reviews

1) *Book*

Buckley, Tom. "Anyone for War?" Rev. of The Long
Gray Line by Rick Atkinson. The New York Times
Book Review 22 Oct. 1989: 18.

2) *Exhibition*

Sherman, Mary. "Expressionist Barlach's Strong,
Solitary Figures." Rev. of Ernst Barlach. Pucker
Safrai Gallery, Boston. Boston Globe 22 Feb.
1990: 76.

3) *Performance*

Kelly, Kevin. "An Open Letter to 'Love Letters.'"
Rev. of Love Letters, by A. R. Gurney. Wilbur
Theater, Boston. Boston Globe 22 Feb. 1990: 73+.

h. Indirect Sources

If you cannot find the original source but must use
material quoted or summarized within another book
(the indirect source), your bibliography card should
give all information available about the original
source. It should also give full information about the
indirect source. All this material will be necessary for
your footnotes. The formal bibliography entry in your
paper will give only the information about the indirect source. For example, on one bibliography card
record both:

a) Broehl, Wayne G. <u>The Molly Maguires</u>.
Cambridge, MA: Harvard University Press,
1964. [**Indirect Source**]
b) Marvin Schegel, <u>Ruler of the Reading: The
Life of Franklin B. Gowan</u>. Harrisburg:
Archives Publishing Co. of Pennsylvania,
1947: 72, qtd. in Broehl 206. [**Direct Source**]

You will include only (a) in the bibliography of your
paper but will need both (a) and (b) for making footnotes. See sample footnote 27 in Section VII:
Preparing The Final Draft.

2. Internet, CD-ROM, and Database Sources

When citing information from the Internet (either files
that you view on your computer screen or those you down-
load), you must give the following pieces of information in
the order below:

- the last name of the author (the author may be an
  organization) of the source followed by a comma,
  then the first name and a period:
  Blum, Harold P.

- the title of the document or of the web page or database (periodical article, short work within a scholarly project, specific database within a larger database)
  in quotation marks with a period inside the closing
  quotation marks:
  Blum, Harold P. **"The Sigmund Freud
  Archive and the Freud Exhibit at the
  Library of Congress."**

- the title of the overall Web site, underlined, followed
  by the name of the editor of the Web site (if available), followed by a period. This information is then

followed by a volume number and/or issue number, if provided, without punctuation:

> Blum, Harold P. "The Sigmund Freud Archive and the Freud Exhibit at the Library of Congress." **Sigmund Freud and the Freud Archives. Ed. Robert Salnave.**

- the date of the work's publication or the date of its most recent revision: day of month followed by month followed by year and by a period:

> Blum, Harold P. "The Sigmund Freud Archive and the Freud Exhibit at the Library of Congress." <u>Sigmund Freud and the Freud Archives</u>. Ed. Robert Salnave. **9 Feb. 1996.**

- the name of any institution or organization sponsoring or associated with the Web site (appropriately abbreviated), followed by a period:

> Blum, Harold P. "The Sigmund Freud Archive and the Freud Exhibit at the Library of Congress." <u>Sigmund Freud and the Freud Archives</u>. Ed. Robert Salnave. 9 Feb. 1996. **The New York Psychoanalytic Inst. and Soc.**

- the full URL (Uniform Resource Locator) address enclosed in angle brackets (i.e., < >), including any hyphens or slashes. In order to retrieve a document from the Internet, you must use the exact URL with no extraneous spaces, missing spaces, or errors in upper/lower case characters:

> Blum, Harold P. "The Sigmund Freud Archive and the Freud Exhibit at the Library of Congress." <u>Sigmund Freud and the Freud Archives</u>. Ed. Robert Salnave. 9 Feb. 1996. The New York Psychoanalytic Inst. and Soc. **<http://plaza.interport.net/nypsan/sfa_loc. html>**

- the date when the researcher viewed the document. Put this date in parentheses, followed by a period. [This instruction is the only way that the writers of WARP have deviated from *MLA Handbook* format.]
    Blum, Harold P. "The Sigmund Freud Archive and the Freud Exhibit at the Library of Congress." <u>Sigmund Freud and the Freud Archives</u>. Ed. Robert Salnave. 9 Feb. 1996. The New York Psychoanalytic Inst. and Soc. <http://plaza.interport.net/nypsan/sfa_loc.html> **(viewed 26 Apr. 1999).**

Examples of Internet citations:

a. Article in a scholarly project
    Blum, Harold P. "The Sigmund Freud Archive and the Freud Exhibit at the Library of Congress." <u>Sigmund Freud and the Freud Archives</u>. Ed. Robert Salnave. 9 Feb. 1996. The New York Psychoanalytic Inst. and Soc. <http://plaza.interport.net/nypsan/sfa_loc.html> (viewed 26 Apr. 1999).

b. Images in a collection
    Antarctic Unit, Tourism Board of Tierra del Fuego. "The Hurley Collection: The British Trans-Antarctic Expedition of 1914/17." <u>Tierra del Fuego: Where America Begins . . .</u> . <http://tierradelfuego.ml.org/antartida/hurleyeng.htm> (viewed 3 May 1999).

c. An individual picture in a collection
    Hurley, Frank. <u>Young Emperor Penguins</u>. "The Hurley Collection: The British Trans-Antarctic Expedition of 1914/17." <u>Tierra del Fuego: Where America Begins . . .</u> . Antarctic Unit, Tourism

Board of Tierra del Fuego. <http://tierradel
fuego.ml.org/antartida/hurleyeng.htm> (viewed 3
May 1999) [Underline the title of a painting, a
photograph, or a sculpture]

d. A database
Cheetham, Robert, ed. "Plant Materials." <u>JGAR-
DEN: Japanese Garden Database</u>. 14 Mar. 1999.
<http://pobox.upenn.edu/~cheetham/jgarden/plants.
html#tree> (viewed 25 Apr. 1999).

e. Government document
United States. Bureau of the Census. "Poverty
1997: People and Families in Poverty by Selected
Characteristics: 1989, 1996, and 1997." <u>Census
Bureau Population Topics and Household
Economic Topics</u>. 3 Feb. 1999.
<http://www.census.gov/hhes/poverty/poverty97/
pv97est1.html> (viewed 21 Apr. 1999).

f. Journal article
James, Jacquelyn B. "The Meanings of Gender."
<u>Gender Matters</u>. Spec. issue of <u>Radcliffe
Quarterly</u>. 84.3 (1998).
<http://www.radcliffe.edu/quarterly/199804/
meanings_gender.html> (viewed 26 Apr. 1999).
[Include page number followed by a period and
the volume or issue number, if relevant]

g. Occasional report
Unicef. "Children in War." Introduction. <u>The State
of the World's Children: 1996</u>.
<http://www.unicef.org/sowc96/intro.htm> (viewed
8 May 1999). [Include Introduction, Preface, or
Afterword, followed by a period, after the title of
the article, if relevant]

h. Posting from a discussion list or online bulletin board
Tremper, Ellen. "Re: Figurative Language Conveys Character's Uncertainties in <u>Mrs. Dalloway</u>." Online posting. 12 Apr. 1997. VWOOLF. <http://www.utoronto.ca/IVWS/listserv.html> (viewed 13 Apr. 1997).

i. E-mail
Vosburgh, Jennett. "Re: WARP." E-mail to Mary Tyler Knowles. 21 Apr. 1999.

j. Radio or television transcript
"Nuclear Espionage?" <u>Online NewsHour with Jim Lehrer</u>. PBS. 30 Apr. 1999. Transcript. <u>Online NewsHour</u>.<http://www.pbs.org/newshour/bb/ asia/jan-june99/richardson_4-30.html> (viewed 2 May 1999).

k. An article from a CD-ROM
Stout, David. "'Safe Rooms' Urged in Areas Prone to Tornadoes." <u>New York Times</u> 19 Aug. 1998, late ed., East Coast: 18. <u>New York Times Ondisc</u>. CD-ROM. UMI-ProQuest. Sept. 1998.
[Note: 18 is the page number. You do not need to give the date viewed because material on a CD-Rom does not change.]

l. Encyclopedia online
"Burbage, Richard." <u>Encyclopaedia Britannica Online</u>. <http://www.eb.com> (viewed 26 Apr. 1999)
[Add version # and date of electronic publication, if available]

m. Periodicals via online subscription services (such

as Ebsco, Electric Library, InfoTrac, ProQuest
Direct, or Lexis-Nexis, etc.)

A work from an online subscription database service
is handled in a special manner:

First, give the information about the print version of
a magazine, journal or newspaper in relevant WARP
format, omitting any facts that are unavailable. Then
give information about the electronic version (articles from CD-ROMs as well as from the Internet).

If page numbers from the printed text are cited in the
database, include them in your entry after the publication date.

Underline the name of the database, but do not
underline the name of the service or the company
that provides the database.

The entry should also include the name of the library
in which you used the database, followed by the city
and, if necessary for clarity, by the state abbrevia-
tion. You need to include the name of the library
because the database may vary with the kind of service a library has paid for. Only by going to the
library named can one be sure to find the article
cited.[2]

Include only a shortened form of the URL of the service's public home page.

For example:

1) Djilas, Aleksa. "A Profile of Slobodan Milosevic."
   Foreign Affairs Summer 1993. Platinum

---

[2]Eric Wirth, "Re[1]; MLA citation form in 5th edition," e-mail to
Mary Tyler Knowles, 4 May 1999.

Periodicals. UMI-ProQuest Direct. Winsor
School Lib., Boston. <http://proquest.umi.com/>
(viewed 21 Apr. 1999).

2) Papert, Seymour. "Child Psychologist: Jean Piaget:
He Found the Secrets of Human Learning and
Knowledge Hidden Behind the Cute and
Seemingly Illogical Notions of Children." Time
29 Mar. 1999: 100. Expanded Academic ASAP.
InfoTrac SearchBank. Winsor School Lib.,
Boston. <http://www.searchbank.com> (viewed 4
May 1999).

3. Other Media

a. Television or Radio Programs
Private Lives, Public Trust. Writ. Stephen Schlow.
Dir. Dimitri Miades. CBS. WHDH, Boston, 27
June 1990.

b. Films
Dracula. Dir. Todd Browning. With Bela Lugosi.
Universal Studios, 1931.

c. Videocassettes or Filmstrips
Hamlet. Videocassette. Dir. Laurence Olivier. With
Olivier. Two Cities Films Ltd., 1948. 155 min.
Based on William Shakespeare's Hamlet.

d. Lectures and Speeches
Perkins, David. "Mrs. Gardner's Circle: T. S. Eliot."
Isabella Stewart Gardner Museum. Boston, 2
Nov. 1989.

e. Interviews
1) *Interview conducted by the researcher*
Greuel, David. Telephone interview. 24 June 1999.

2) *Interview from a radio or television program*
Dove, John. "Training for the Boston Marathon for College Credit." <u>All Things Considered</u>. By David Wright. National Public Radio. WGBH, Boston, 15 Apr. 1991.

f. Works of Art
1) *Exhibited painting*
Monet, Claude. <u>Rouen Cathedral Façade</u>. Museum of Fine Arts, Boston.
2) *Photograph of a painting*
Monet, Claude. <u>La Cathédrale de Rouen</u>. National Gallery of Art, Washington, DC. P. 174 in <u>Monet</u>. By Robert Gordon and Andrew Forge. New York: Abrams, 1984.

D. SPECIFIC DIRECTIVES FOR WRITING BIBLIOGRAPHY CARDS

1. If an article or book is unsigned, start the bibliography entry with the title. (*See 1.c.2*)
2. If a pamphlet does not appear at regular intervals, treat it like a book; however, treat a pamphlet published at regular intervals like a magazine.
3. a. For a magazine, put the inverted date (26 Feb. 1990) right after the title of the magazine, followed by a colon and the page numbers (31) ending with a period. Abbreviate all months except May, June, and July. (*See 1.e.2*)
b. For a journal, give the volume number after the title, then the date in parentheses, followed by a colon and page numbers as above. (*See 1.e.3*)
4. If more than one city is given for a publisher, use the first one.
5. When dealing with republications:
a. If a book has been revised, write the number of the

edition you are using immediately after the title, ending with a period. Follow this sentence with the usual publication information. (*See 1.d.3*)

b. If a book has been reprinted, give the original publication date, followed by a period, immediately after the title. Then give publication information for the work you are using. (*See 1.d.1*)

6. **a**. The formal bibliography entry for an encyclopedia article requires only the author, title of article, title of encyclopedia, date and/or edition. BUT on your bibliography card, note also the volume and page number of the article you consulted because you will need this information for your footnotes. Note that many articles are signed only with initials which are identified elsewhere in the encyclopedia. (*See 1.c.1 & 1.c.2 and bibliography sample card for encyclopedia entry.*)

b. When using a dictionary as a source, follow the form for an encyclopedia entry. (*See 1.c.1 & 1.c.2, etc.*)

7. If there is more than one group responsible for a government document, put the larger group first, the smaller group second, etc. (*See f.1.b.*)

8. When making references to the Bible, cite the book of the Bible (abbreviated), chapter and verse, but never a page number (Ex: Gen. 1:16-20). Specify the version of the Bible used (Ex: King James, American Revised, etc.).

IV
Making Card Notes

A. TAKING NOTES

Once you have established that there is a range of reliable and accessible information on your subject, you will begin to take notes. You will need 3 x 5 cards and a protective container for them. Alternatively, computer programs for note taking exist and are increasingly useful; such programs allow the researcher to record and categorize data and to call it up again in the original categories or in cross-referenced categories. Whether one uses a computer or an index card system, one must learn the fundamental skill of setting up categories appropriate to the data.

As you read, note the facts, ideas, and opinions relevant to your topic on the cards or in your computer program. The note taking stage of the paper is a very important one, for the accuracy with which you read and the discrimination you show in choosing data appropriate to support and develop your topic will determine the quality of the content of your final paper.

Enter a single piece of information on each card. Although this process may seem inefficient at this stage, it will facilitate the organization of your paper later. If you put just one item of information on each card, you will then have freedom to organize your material as your paper begins to develop. Because you will undoubtedly need to redefine and refocus your limited topic as your research progresses, the flexibility provided for reorganization by recording *one bit of data per card* is crucial.

Here is a model card followed by an explanation of it:

<u>Labor of monks—reduced</u>   DB 222 Servants in monasteries often equaled, sometimes exceeded, number of monks.

1. At the upper right of each card be sure to include a code which identifies author (by initial of last name) and book (by initial of title) and the *page number* from which the information is taken. This information will be crucial for footnotes later on.
2. On the upper left of each note card, write a topical heading for the natural division of the subject under which the note falls. While it is not always possible to create headings early in the research process, and while you may not know the final divisions of your paper at first, be sure to create headings after you have written about twenty note cards. For an eight- to ten-page paper, you will probably narrow down to ten or fewer final headings. For example, the writer of the student essay in Appendix A used the following categories to organize and identify the material for her paper: Fixed games in baseball before 1919; Comiskey, Charles; White Sox players; Landis, Judge Kennesaw; World Series 1919. If you are using a computer note-card system, remember to include similarly appropriate key words which will enable you to call up related data easily.
3. Once again, *make only one entry on each note card.* Write notes concisely; use fragments, full sentences, or direct quotations as seems appropriate.
4. *Use quotations marks* whenever you quote the exact words of a source even if you are recording just a phrase in the author's own words.
5. Do not number note cards. Their order will certainly change as you organize your paper.

6. Use only one side of each note card so that you can look over your note cards quickly and see the extent of information under each heading.

7. Write notes in ink because pencil fades.

B. CORRECT AND INCORRECT NOTE TAKING TECHNIQUES

1. Limiting information

Right:

<u>Labor of monks—limited</u>	CFI 175
Monks did only writing, manuscript copying, and crafts.	

Wrong:

<u>Labor—St. Benedict</u>	BR 85
St. Benedict said: work in fields is blessing for monks. Work in fields, cleaning, cooking done by hired servants. St. Benedict: "idleness is an enemy of the soul."	

Not even the heading of the second card is appropriately limited, nor does it specify the relationship between the topic "Labor" and the man "St. Benedict." The material could be separated onto several note cards, two of which might be headed "<u>Labor: Attitude of St. Benedict.</u>" One card might say "St. Benedict calls work in the fields a blessing for monks" while the other card might read "St. Benedict states: 'Idleness is an enemy of the soul.'" Be sure to record material accurately. If the source made a cause/effect statement about the lack of hard labor by monks, the note needs to reflect that idea: for example, "Lack of hard labor by monks harmful to spiritual atmosphere of the monastery."

2. Choosing whether to quote or to paraphrase

When you take down factual information, direct quotation will rarely be necessary. The record of a date, a name, or a place can probably be stated simply in your own words. Summarizing an author's opinion on an issue is often another matter, however. Be sure to quote directly any words which show an author's distinctive attitude or point of view. In the following examples, note the rhetorical nature of the question as well as the satirical tone. John of Oyton must be quoted directly in order to preserve both.

Right:

Monastic gluttony   CFI
392

John of Oyton's attitude
"Which, I ask, is the graver transgression in the matter of flesh-eating? That of the Black monks [Benedictines], who eat it openly, or of the White monks [Cistercians], who often eat it secretly to repletion? For both have the same Benedictine Rule."

Wrong:

Monastic gluttony   CFI 392
John of Oyton, 14th century economist, wonders whether Black or White monks are worse for eating flesh since one group does it openly and the other secretly.

3. Deciding the number of note cards to use

There should be a proportionate number of note cards for each source. Twenty cards, for example, from five pages of one book and a mere ten more cards from four other sources might indicate a lack of balance in your research. If you discover more than one source corroborating an important statement, you might record the code identification and page reference for each corroborating source on the initial card. This procedure will enable you to demonstrate that a fact, idea, or conclusion is indeed part of common knowledge. Although the total number of cards may vary, for a final paper of approximately eight pages you will need a minimum of seventy-five cards from which to work.

C. AVOIDING PLAGIARISM

There are two kinds of plagiarism: claiming an author's ideas, including the organization, as your own and using his or her words without acknowledgment. Intentional plagiarism is deliberately dishonest; unintentional plagiarism, while not deliberately dishonest, is nevertheless blameworthy.

Unintentional plagiarism often occurs because of

improper note taking. If you take verbatim any words from a source, be sure to copy them on your note card accurately, to enclose them in quotation marks, and to give the exact source. Follow this procedure in taking notes whether you copy a whole section, a sentence, or just a striking phrase or word. If you do not take notes carefully, you are likely to transfer the words from the note to the first draft and then to the final copy without remembering to give credit to the actual author. Unless you want an exact quotation for a specific reason (see IV B 2), the safest procedure is to take notes completely in your own words.

An original passage and examples of four types of plagiarism of it appear below:

Original passage

. . . Social futurism must cut even deeper. For technocrats suffer from more than econo-think and myopia; they suffer, too, from the virus of elitism. To capture control of change, we shall, therefore, require a final, even more radical break away from technocratic tradition: we shall need a revolution in the very way we formulate our social goals.

Rising novelty renders irrelevant the traditional goals of our chief institutions—state, church, corporation, army and university. Acceleration produces a faster turnover of goals, a greater transience of purpose. Diversity or fragmentation leads to a relentless multiplication of goals. Caught in the churning, goal-cluttered environment, we stagger future shocked, from crisis to crisis, pursuing a welter of conflicting and self-cancelling purposes.

Nowhere is this more starkly evident than in our pathetic attempts to govern our cities. New Yorkers, within a short span, have suffered a nightmarish succession of near disasters: a water shortage, a subway strike, racial violence in the schools, a student insurrection at Columbia University, a garbage strike, a housing shortage, a fuel oil strike, a breakdown of telephone service, a teacher walkout, a power blackout, to name just a few. In New York's City Hall, as in a thousand city halls all over the high-technology nations, technocrats dash, firebucket in fist, from one conflagration to another without the least semblance of a coherent plan or policy for the urban future.[3]

EXAMPLES OF PLAGIARISM

1. Word-for-word plagiarism

Social futurism must cut even deeper. To avoid the virus of elitism and to capture control of change, we require a radical breakaway from technocratic tradition and a revolution in the way we formulate our social goals. Now we stagger, future shocked, from crisis to crisis, pursuing a welter of conflicting and self-cancelling purposes and in a thousand city halls all over the high-technology nations, technocrats dash, firebucket in fist, from one conflagration to another without the least semblance of a coherent plan or policy for the urban future.

This plagiarism might well be the result of having copied sentences from Toffler onto note cards and then putting them together in the paragraph. If the writer had enclosed all the copied text in quotation marks and had identified the source in a footnote, he or she would not be liable to

---

[3] Alvin Toffler, *Future Shock* (New York: Random House, Inc. 1970) 403. Quoted by permission of Random House, Inc.

the charge of plagiarism; however, a reader might feel justifiably that the writer's personal contribution to the discussion was not very significant.

2. The mosaic

> We are faced with a serious crisis in the Twentieth-Century society and need to capture control of the change that surrounds us. We need a revolution in the way we formulate our social goals. Cities like New York (which has, in a short span, faced a nightmarish succession of near disasters ranging from racial violence to a power blackout) stagger from crisis to crisis without the least semblance of a plan or policy for their urban futures.

In the mosaic, phrases have been moved out of their original order and arranged in new patterns. There is really no way to make this mosaic legitimate, for to put every stolen phrase within quotation marks would produce an almost unreadable, and quite worthless, text.

3. The apt term

In the following passage the writer has not been able to resist the appropriation of two striking terms—"the virus of elitism" and "churning, goal-cluttered environment."

> The problems caused by rapid and perplexing change must be dealt with in our society. In solving these problems we must be aware that technocrats on whom we might wish to depend are often committed to rigid economic theories and, moreover, suffer from the virus of elitism. They too are caught in this churning, goal-cluttered environment and thus cannot lead us towards the revision of our social goals that we so desperately need.

A perfectly proper use of the terms would be:

> The problems caused by rapid and perplexing change must be dealt with in our society. In solving these problems we must be aware that technocrats on whom we might wish to depend are often committed to rigid economic theories, and, moreover, in Alvin Toffler's phrase, suffer from "the virus of elitism." They too are caught in what Toffler calls the "churning, goal-cluttered environment" and thus cannot lead us towards the revision of our social goals that we so desperately need.

Terms like "technocrat" and "social goals" are so common that they do not need attribution.

4. Plagiarism of the idea

Even the second paragraph in Example 3 must be footnoted to give full information as to the source of ideas in the passage.

> Since one of the principles of an education is the development of intellectual honesty, it is obvious that plagiarism is a particularly serious offense and the punishment for it is commensurately severe. What a penalized student suffers can never really be known by anyone else; what the student who plagiarizes and "gets away with it" suffers is less public and probably less acute, but the corruptness of the act, the disloyalty and baseness it entails, must inevitably leave an ineradicable mark on the individual as well as on the institution of which he or she is privileged to be a member.[4]

---

[4] Much of the preceding material in IV C except for the examples, is quoted from Harold C. Martin and Richard M. Ohman, *The Logic and Rhetoric of Exposition*. Revised Edition. (New York: Holt, Rinehart and Winston, 1964) 275-278. Quoted by permission of Holt, Rinehart and Winston.

THE WRITING PROCESS

V
Planning the Paper

A. GETTING STARTED

Planning a paper is a creative process. You will need to work on your thesis statement and your outline concurrently. It is generally useful to begin with a tentative thesis statement.

B. WRITING A THESIS STATEMENT

A thesis is a one or two sentence statement which expresses the basic idea a paper will develop. Writing the thesis is a crucial step in the preparation of any paper because the thesis determines focus, length, and type of organization of the paper.

A GOOD THESIS IS RESTRICTED, PRECISE, AND UNIFIED.

1. Restriction

The thesis must indicate which of several approaches to the subject the writer will take. It thus limits the scope of the paper to what can be properly discussed in the space available. For example, such a thesis as "The Japanese Relocation Camps set up in the early 1940s had many effects on the people detained in them" is vague because it does not specify what particular effects the author will discuss.

Notice that the following thesis clearly states which effects will be discussed and thus restricts the writer to something that may be explained fairly thoroughly in 2500 words:

> The Japanese Relocation Camps set up in the early 1940s had the short-term effect of making the Japanese Americans intensify their patriotism to prove their loyalty to the United States and the long-term effect of breaking family traditions and causing poverty.

The unrestricted thesis gives the reader no real clue to what the author plans to write and often makes the writer think the purpose is clear when he or she has little more than a general subject. An unrestricted thesis invites vague thinking, meandering organization, and superficiality.

2. Precision

A thesis should be phrased in words which permit only one interpretation. Especially, it should avoid words and phrases that are so general that they convey no exact meaning. "Organic gardening is an interesting hobby" or "Winston Churchill had a colorful career" are useless as thesis statements because the key words "interesting" and "colorful" could mean almost anything. If you intend to write "about" a subject, you have not yet established your purpose. You have merely lulled yourself into a false sense of achievement by the vagueness of your words. In a thesis, precise use of words is more important than effect.

3. Unity

To be unified, a thesis must commit the writer to investigate only one dominant idea. Such a thesis as "Hitler made serious tactical errors and refused to listen to his generals" requires the writer to do two things, not one. A paper with this double purpose will almost certainly fall into two parts having little connection with each other. "Because Hitler thought his generals were conspiring against him, he refused to heed their advice, and therefore made a series of major tactical errors" is a thesis that fuses the two parts into a unified purpose statement.

Another example:

Co-educational colleges grew rapidly in 1970s America and fulfilled a social need. (not unified)

Co-educational colleges grew rapidly in 1970s America because they fulfilled a social need. (unified)

Beware of the use of *and* in a thesis statement as a coordinating conjunction between two independent clauses, for *and* often signals that you have not carefully considered the relationships between your ideas. Other connectors that do provide a logical relationship between ideas are:

when, after, until, while	(time)
because, as, whereas, since	(explanation or cause)
in order that, so that, that	(purpose)
although, if, while, even though	(condition)
on the one hand . . . on the other hand, but, yet, however, nevertheless	(contrast)
consequently, therefore, as a result	(result)
not only . . . but also	(parallel addition)

4. The choice of the logical connectors in the thesis forecasts the organizational structure of the essay

If your essay is to be a comparison/contrast essay, you might select connectors such as *but, on the one hand . . . on the other hand.* If your essay is to be an analysis of the causes of an event, you might select the *because* or the *in order to* connectors. (Example: "Aquaculture flourishes in many areas of the world today because wild stocks of fish and mollusks have been depleted at the same time that demand for seafood has risen.")

If your essay will contain a section dealing with a condition that needs exploring and explaining in relation to the main idea, you might select an *although* connector. For example, "Although Mahler's innovations in symphonic form were ignored or misunderstood by the critics of his era, they are today recognized as one of his greatest achievements." Such an essay would focus primarily on the main clause but would also provide for an introductory section on Mahler's critics' ignoring what has come to be so highly regarded by modern-day critics. Similarly, such a thesis as "Although Charlotte Brontë wrote under a pseudonym, she was not afraid to tackle problems of women who were exploited by society" allows one to focus in on the main topic of Charlotte Brontë as social critic through an introductory discussion of how her use of a pseudonym reveals her to be the victim of a male-dominated society.

5. Two basic methods of organization

Rhetorical Induction—the process of examining instances to find in them generalizations that are acceptable.
Rhetorical Deduction—the process in which the writer begins with a generalization and through analysis of its parts and of specific examples verifies its truth.

Example of a paragraph organized inductively:

If you do not mind having an aching back and dirty fingernails; if you prefer a sunburnt neck and hands to an even tan; if you can spend Monday combatting potato bugs and aphids and return on Tuesday to make war against Japanese beetles; if you refuse to go to the beach on the hottest weekend of the year because the first tomato is due to ripen—you have the makings of a gardener in you. Of course you will soon become aware that your garden is both a millstone and an obsession, but all that will not matter the day you pick your first cool, green cucumber. When you eat the first green beans or zucchini or corn, backaches and bugs will be seen in their true perspective. *You will realize that gardening is a strenuous, frustrating but ultimately satisfying activity.*

Example of a paragraph organized deductively:

Birthday celebrations are joyous nightmares. Fondly we remember that childhood birthday party, the multi-colored dripping popsicles, the sticky icing on our fingers, the blobs of wax from melting candles on the special party cloth. Happily we recall playing "pin-the-tail-on-the-donkey" and "musical chairs" and even the screams of anger when we did not win the prize. The day was our day; we were the center of attention and we still are at our adult birthday celebrations. There are still gifts and occasionally party hats and streamers. But the table cloth is white and neat now and the silver gleaming and the voices more subdued, and in the course of the "happy birthday" song we think of the passing of time and covertly watch the faces around us, wondering whether we too so obviously show our age. And then we know that we would gladly trade this polite and ordered celebration for the joyous "nightmare" of our childhood birthday party.

Notice the placement of the italicized topic sentence in each paragraph.

In a longer paper the thesis statement will naturally

be more complex than the topic sentences of the above paragraphs. The following thesis suggests a paper divided into three sections of approximately equal length:

> The childish stories she invented with her siblings, her attentive readings of Byron, and her intense love of the Yorkshire landscape all prepared Emily Brontë to write her masterpiece *Wuthering Heights*.

Notice that the order provides for an initial chronological approach and places the most general idea last. The reasoning in the paper will probably be inductive.

> Heathcliff in *Wuthering Heights* and Mr. Rochester in *Jane Eyre* are both examples of the Gothic hero, but Heathcliff is an amoral devil while Rochester is merely a slightly immoral man.

This thesis suggests a definition section followed by compare/contrast development. This working from a generalization to an examination of particular cases is deductive. While many writers prefer to place the thesis of an essay in the first paragraph and to work deductively, most topics can be handled equally well by either method of organization.

C. MAKING THE OUTLINE

1. Indicate main section topics

When you know your subject thoroughly and have developed a tentative thesis statement, it is time to make a tentative outline for the paper. Read through all of your note cards and sort them into the major divisions which correspond to the major divisions of your thesis statement. There are usually three to five of these divisions. If your note cards do not correspond to the thesis statement, you must stop to revise your thesis or to collect more data. After you have sorted the cards into major divisions, write a section sentence for each of the major divisions. These main divisions usually are equal in importance. Also, the structure of the section sentences should be parallel. Arrange these main section sentences in a logical order and number them with Roman numerals. (I, II, etc.)

2. Indicate subsections or paragraph topics

Read through each major division of cards to discover subsections. Each subsection will be a paragraph in your essay. Create a topic sentence that corresponds to each subsection. Arrange these topic sentences in a logical order and number them with capital letters, preceded by the appropriate Roman numeral. (IA, IB, etc.) Although you will include many details in support of each paragraph topic sentence in your essay, you do not need to indicate these paragraph details in your outline. Be sure, however, that you have a sufficient number of cards providing details for each paragraph. If you discover your information to be inadequate, look up additional details.

3. The form of the outline

Keep the following points in mind:

a. Label your outline sections in the following way: Roman numerals for section sentences, capital letters for paragraph topic sentences. (Were you to include paragraph examples, they would be labeled with Arabic numerals; details of the examples would be labeled with lowercase letters.)

b. Each section sentence contains one part of the thesis statement. Each paragraph topic sentence presents one part of the section sentence.

c. Both section topics and paragraph subtopics *must* be expressed in full sentences to show completed ideas.

d. Each section must contain at least two paragraph subtopics. That is, if you have an *A*, you must have a *B*.

e. Keep your outline as simple as possible. Be sure that sections are equally important in content and roughly comparable in length.

f. *Be sure to write on one side of the sheet only* so that you can see the entire structure at a glance.

g. You must include your thesis statement at the top of your outline.

4. Sample outline

Thesis Statement: Although the institution of monasticism contributed greatly to medieval life through a distribution of charity and the atmosphere of learning and culture which surrounded it, the daily life of the individual monastery was often rendered corrupt by the frequent bypassing, by both the abbots and the monastic community in general, of the traditions and the way of life established by St. Benedict's Rule.

I. Medieval society benefited from the presence of the monasteries because of the charity and hospitality they distributed to the poor and travelers, and because of the many intellectual and cultural contributions they had to offer.

  A. According to monastic tradition, the monks offered charity by means of guesthouses and meals to the poor and to travelers, thus benefiting much of the population.

  B. The monasteries were also great centers for intellectual and cultural growth; the monks were among the most educated people in the world, and they initiated a great many of the important advances in literature, architecture, and music.

II. The abbot, the most important member of the monastic community was gradually forced to relinquish his role as the father of the community; in order to fulfill his obligations as a feudal lord, he could no longer live as an ordinary monk nor set a good example to his fellow monks.

A. As his monastery began to possess more and more land and as his feudal and administrative responsibilities increased, the medieval abbot found himself to be increasingly estranged from the ordinary life of his abbey.

B. Since the abbot was the very "pivot on which the life of the monastery turned," if he were a strong, spiritual man, the monastery would follow suit, but, conversely, if he were either weak, or highly secular, the monks could do (and did) as they pleased.

III. The high ideals set forth in the monastic Rules were often rendered corrupt by not being followed word for word and were sometimes abandoned almost entirely.

A. Since they followed the secular example set by the abbots, it was a common sight to see monks wandering through the medieval countryside, a direct affront to St. Benedict's Rule, which dictates strict confinement to the monastery.

B. Ignoring the precept of poverty, which implies a complete renunciation of personal property, most medieval monks had possessions, ranging from costume jewelry to slaves, and varying amounts of money.

C. By tradition and St. Benedict's Rule, butcher's meat was forbidden to the monks except under certain conditions such as sickness or meals with guests, and eating was, at all times, to be in moderation; in actuality, however, monks were commonly satirized as gluttons, and meat was a standard part of their diet.

D. In disregard of the old Benedictine principle *ora et* *labora*, pray and work, virtually all monks had ceased any heavy manual labor by the medieval period and were primarily idle.

E. The sexual immorality of the monks, while not universal, nor as widespread as some of the other corruptions mentioned above, still existed to a significant degree; the fact that it existed at all is disturbing.

5. Omit introduction and conclusion in the outline

Every completed essay must contain both an introduction and a conclusion, yet these labels should be omitted when you outline an essay. Only the logical structure and the factual content of an essay, not its stylistic devices, are included in the outline. (See further discussion of Introduction and Conclusion in Chapter VI B and C.)

VI
Writing the First Draft

A. USE OF NOTE CARDS AND OUTLINE TO DEVELOP THE FIRST DRAFT

You have gathered information while doing research and taking note cards, and you have thought through the logical structure of the paper while making the outline. The first draft is the step in which you fill in the outline. To write the first draft, all you need are your note cards and your outline; no books should be used.

Check over the ordering of note cards, which you sorted according to headings while planning the outline. Make sure (1) that each card is useful for its subsection, (2) that you are not keeping some cards because they are too interesting to set aside even if they are irrelevant, and (3) that you have enough information to develop each subsection fully.

The outline presents the order of ideas in your paper. Sentences for major sections in the outline (I, II, etc.) do not appear as topic sentences for separate paragraphs, but they may be adapted for use as transitions. Each subsection heading (IA, IB, etc.) presents the main idea for one paragraph. Thus, IA is the main idea for the first paragraph after the introduction; IB is the main idea for the paragraph after that. Beside each paragraph in the first draft, write the number and letter of the subsection in the outline which it develops. Develop the main idea for each paragraph fully with facts and explanations. Unsubstantiated generalizations are not acceptable; solid, well-developed paragraphs will make your paper convincing.

B. THE INTRODUCTION

Because the introduction is the first paragraph (or paragraphs) in the paper, it must serve at least four functions. First, it should catch the reader's attention. A striking fact, a question, a provocative quotation, a brief anecdote are among the devices you might use to engage the reader's attention. Second, the introduction should indicate the subject of the paper. In a paper with a deductive structure, the introduction might state the central idea; in a paper with an inductive structure, it might pose the question which the paper will ultimately answer or delineate which area of the subject will be discussed. The third function of the introduction is to establish the tone of the paper—the attitude of the author toward subject and reader, and the level of formality. In most essays the tone will tend to be formal, but it should not be stiff. Finally, the introduction serves to give brief but necessary background information.

Were you writing your essay, for example, on Charlotte Brontë's struggle to become a novelist, you might introduce the subject with a brief anecdote of how Charlotte Brontë went to the publishing company, Smith, Elder & Co., that had accepted *Jane Eyre*. The publishers, expecting a man because she had written the novel under a male pseudonym, Currier Bell, were startled to see a small, rather dumpy female enter their office. You might follow this anecdote with questions: What caused Charlotte Brontë to assume a pseudonym? Did her unprepossessing size and use of a false name reveal timidity, or did they cloak and protect her aggressiveness? Such questions would prepare for an exploration of the cultural milieu in which Charlotte Brontë wrote. This anecdotal method will engage the reader's attention and establish a focus for background information.

If you decide to begin with a quotation, you might proceed in the following manner: For an essay dealing with the Borgias' abuse of power, this quotation from Shakespeare, "Boundless intemperance/In nature is a tyranny. It hath been/The untimely emptying of the happy throne,/And fall of many kings" (*Macbeth*. IV. iii. 67-70) serves to catch the reader's attention, to establish the theme of the essay, and to convey the attitude of the author toward the subject.

Because the thesis of the problem-centered essay in Appendix C is stated in its conclusion, the function of its introduction is, first, to establish a context, an overview, for all that follows. Second, it delineates the specific focus of the essay (see the last sentence of the introductory paragraph). And, third, it stimulates the reader's interest by indicating that a conventional view of the subject material is, in fact, incorrect.

The Age of Faith, The Golden Age of Monasticism— epithets that are commonly applied to the European Middle Ages. They evoke in our minds a time of great Christian feeling, a time when the lives of most people revolved around the Church, and when a person of deep religious convictions naturally gravitated toward life in a monastic community, living piously in prayer and holy labor. Not so, for most inhabitants of medieval monasteries were not the devout and devoted individuals we often consider them to be; many were younger sons of nobles, with family property entailed away from them by primogeniture, who had no choice but to enter a monastery. Others were noble bastards, whose fathers wished them out of the way at a minimum expense, or criminals, for whom the tonsure was an alternative to prison.[1] Consequently, the pious and holy ideals of monastic life were very often set aside, the monks seeming to be rather members of a "rich bachelor fraternity"[2] than the spiritual and self-denying men they were supposed to be. In spite of the general irreligious atmosphere and the many infractions of the monastic Rules, however, the overall influence of the many abbeys and priories was positive, for they provided the opportunity to learn and study in a society where intellectual knowledge was usually secondary (especially among the lower classes) to physical prowess. The monks were also the medieval equivalent of a welfare and hostel system: they distributed alms and food to the needy and poor, and the monastery guest house was the temporary home of many travelers. The façade of the monasteries of Medieval Europe is that of a solid institution that benefited society. A closer look, however, reveals the many corruptions with which it was riddled. The gradual decline from the grand monastic tradition of St. Benedict's Rule, the first and greatest of the monastic Rules, and the secularization which accompanied it were typical of medieval monachism.

For two quite different techniques, see the introductions of the papers in Appendixes A and B.

C. THE CONCLUSION

A paper reaches its substantive conclusion when it has answered the questions or resolved the problem initially stated. The substantive conclusion is thus part of the main content of the paper. The stylistic conclusion, on the other hand, is that which comes after the substantive conclusion and is thus in a position of emphasis. Although some papers will omit the stylistic conclusion, all papers must contain a substantive conclusion.

Because readers are likely to remember what the substantive conclusion says, be sure this last paragraph includes what you want them to retain. You might choose to include your thesis in the concluding paragraph, especially if your essay focused on a problem or began by asking a question; even in a factual paper, you might put your thesis at the end. For example, here is the conclusion of the student's paper on the World Series Scandal of 1919 found in Appendix A:

> Thus, because fixed games existed long before 1919, because team owner Charles Comiskey paid his players unfairly, and because some of the players who disapproved of the scheme, nevertheless, did not want to be excluded from it, eight members of the Chicago White Sox agreed to lose the World Series of 1919. This scandal threatened the future of baseball until 1921, when baseball's first commissioner, Judge Landis, imposed severe punishments on the eight players in an effort to convince angry fans that he was purifying the game. In a way, the scandal of 1919 was inevitable because of the prevalence of corruption and the weakness of baseball's officials. Fortunately, Landis became involved in the situation. Some people argue that Landis's punishments, particularly of Weaver and Jackson, were too harsh. But Landis was correct. Had he allowed Jackson and Weaver to continue playing, he probably would not have convinced fans that baseball was once again clean. Landis needed to prove that he would not allow any player even remotely associated with corruption to stay in the game. Landis also sent the message to other players that he would tolerate no further corruption. Thus, President Taft was correct in stating baseball was a "clean, straight, game." It never had been before, but because Landis intervened, he saved the game from self-destructing.

In writing a stylistic conclusion, you might restate the main point in an interesting and fresh way, or you might indicate the significance of what you have shown in the essay. The conclusion should also give your readers a sense of completion, of coming to an end. Reminding the readers of the opening paragraph by repetition of a key word, phrase, or idea will bring them to see how much they have learned since then. Oftentimes if you have begun with an anecdote, you might end by concluding it. For example, in the essay on Charlotte Brontë, the writer might conclude that the publishers, although dismayed at their first sight of Charlotte Brontë, found her not a prudish, provincial little woman but a high-spirited, mordant critic of social institutions. A well-chosen quotation might also sum up the thrust of the paper. For example, here is the conclusion of a student's paper on Eugene Victor Debs:

> So Eugene Victor Debs, who began his fight for working class rights as a reformer, became a revolutionary. As head of the American Railway Union, he wished to bring capital and labor closer together, but as a socialist he wished to overthrow the capitalist class. The capitalists themselves, in trying to subdue Debs, brought about this change. Capitalism thought it had destroyed Debs; it had merely made him. Debs's own statement is the best summary of this change. "I have tried the step-at-a-time policy, I have been an opportunist, but after years of experience and work and agitation, gentlemen, I have landed on a bedrock of socialism and from that I will not move."

D. ACKNOWLEDGMENT OF SOURCES

Much of any research paper is based on sources. Acknowledge these sources; that is, state in a footnote, endnote, or parenthetical citation within your text where you found a particular piece of data. The purposes of such acknowledgment are (1) to enable the reader to pursue an interesting idea or fact further, and (2) to give credit to the person whose work you have read. To claim someone else's work as your own is dishonest. To fail to give credit out of carelessness is both undisciplined and dishonest.

"But," you may say, "then everything in my paper will be credited to someone else." The organization, style, and conclusions will be your own, but you will, indeed, have many citations. You must give the source for the following:

a direct quotation
an indirect quotation
an opinion or conclusion not originally yours
a statistic or result of a study
a distinctive form of organization
a fact not part of common knowledge

As a general rule, a fact is considered part of common knowledge if you have found it in three different sources: for example, that Benjamin Franklin's original trade was printing. A less well-known fact, such as the weight of the world's smallest mushroom, or a controversial fact, such as the wisdom of the bombing of Hiroshima, should be credited. If a whole paragraph in your paper is based on ideas from a source, put a footnote at the end of the paragraph indicating that source. As you gain more experience, you will develop surer judgment about when to credit sources, but remember the rule, *when in doubt, footnote.*

E. CITATIONS IN THE FIRST DRAFT

In the first draft put all citations in parentheses right after the material to be cited. Cite the code for author (first initial of last name) and title (first initial of title), and the page number. Here is an example based on the student paper in Appendix A:

> In 1918, Comiskey once again refused to discuss salary changes, and the White Sox threatened to strike (AE 21).

Do not number your citations, for their order may change as you revise sections of your paper.

F. EVEN MORE CONSIDERATIONS FOR THE FIRST DRAFT

1. Use only one side of each sheet of paper, and use every other or every third line. Also leave substantial margins on each side. These procedures will leave space for rewriting and editing.
2. Keep the different sections in proportion to each other, not too much space devoted to one section and too little to another.
3. Use the third person and an objective style throughout. Avoid all use of *I* or *me* or *my* or *you*. Leave yourself out of the paper.
4. Avoid the passive voice; not "This was said by Kennedy . . . ," but "Kennedy in the first debate with Nixon said that. . . ."
5. You must key your paper to your outline. To show what part of the outline each paragraph develops, immediately before each paragraph put a Roman numeral to indicate the section and a capital letter to indicate the subsection, e.g., IA.
6. When submitting the first draft, include a copy of the final thesis statement and outline as approved by the teacher. You may have found that as you wrote the first draft, you needed to make some changes in the order of your paper. Revise the outline so it agrees with the

paper, and submit this revised outline with your paper also.

G. PROOFREADING AND REVISING THE FIRST DRAFT

Once you have written a complete first draft, you should go through it critically and revise it in order to make it as strong as possible. Writing is a craft and takes much deliberate effort. This means that before handing the paper in to the teacher, you may have to rewrite a large part of the draft or revise some parts a number of times. You should add, eliminate, or rearrange material where appropriate. You will probably have to rewrite and edit sentences, paragraphs, or even whole sections. Sometimes you may decide to move a section to an entirely different place in the essay. Make your revisions clearly, fully, and legibly so that the teacher can understand easily what you have written and so that you will remember what you meant when you are writing the final draft.

You should consider the following points when revising. Go over the list, note areas in which you tend to be weak, and then check through your first draft, looking especially for those trouble spots.

Paragraphs:

1. Is there a single paragraph for each subtopic in the outline?
2. Is each paragraph clearly and logically organized?
3. Does all the material in the paragraph relate to the topic sentence?
4. Excluding the paragraphs of introduction and conclusion, does the first draft have the same number of paragraphs as there are capital letters in the outline?

Development:

1. Are specific facts, details, and examples used in order to avoid unsubstantiated generalizing?
2. Has the significance of the evidence been explained?
3. Does each section present both an adequate and a concise treatment of its subject?

Grammar and Mechanics:

1. Check your work for errors of grammar. Are there problems of subject-verb agreement, dangling or misplaced modifiers, faulty parallelism, incorrect or vague reference, faulty subordination, inaccurate comparisons, incorrect pronoun reference or case? You should obtain and use a grammar handbook.
2. Check your work for errors in word choice and usage. Have you confused words such as *affect-effect* or *imply-infer*?
3. Check your work for punctuation errors. Are there any run-on sentences, comma splices, or fragments? Have you used quotation marks, commas, and semicolons accurately? Here is another instance in which a grammar handbook is invaluable.
4. Check your spelling. Have you availed yourself of a dictionary, an electronic spell-checker, or a word processing spell-check program?

Style:

1. Are the introduction and conclusion strong and interesting?
2. Is the style appropriately objective and consistent throughout? Does it avoid slang, colloquialisms, contractions, and reference to self?
3. Are sentences varied in pattern and length?
4. Is the writing concise? Could material be combined and

relationships be indicated by coordination or subordination? Could some materials or wordiness be struck out?

5. Are there valid transitions from one point to another within paragraphs, from one paragraph to another, from one main division to another? (See Section VII A for an example of a weak and an improved transition.)

6. Are sources acknowledged when appropriate?

VII
Preparing the Final Draft

A. REVISION OF THE FIRST DRAFT

In some courses the teacher or instructor will read the entire first draft of your paper, commenting in detail only on one or two sections and on the introduction and conclusion. This procedure requires you to apply criticism independently to the uncorrected sections of your paper.

You may, however, be entirely on your own as you come to the last step of the writing process. Whether you have had the benefit of another reader's comments or have had to be your own critic, take your time and try to see your work objectively.

Before you begin to write the final draft, read through the entire paper carefully; identify and categorize mistakes and weaknesses in grammar, rhetoric, and style. Then correct and revise one section at a time, being careful to look for identified weaknesses in the uncorrected sections. Make all necessary corrections and revisions on the first draft before preparing the final copy.

The following paragraphs come from the promising first draft of a student essay on whether apes have the ability to learn language as humans do. Although the student researched her subject thoroughly, she has created a kind of "wastebasket paragraph"; that is, she begins with a topic sentence (underlined) and tosses in related ideas from her notecards without explaining clearly the significance of the material. The teacher points out that the student needs to make her point more directly and to improve the connections between ideas.

> . . . Until the apes begin to converse appropriately as children do, most experts will not consider their signing to be a form of human language.

[margin note: more of a transition ceded here →]

(III B) <u>The apes created sign combinations that varied in order and that never increased in complexity, demonstrating the lack of a child's ability to learn to make more complicated utterances and, even more significantly, the lack of a child's sense of language's structure.</u> In human language, a sentence represents a complete idea through a group of words that have specific grammatical relations. These relations, unlike the words themselves, cannot be learned individually; they constitute a part of the *grammar* of the language. ⟨Psycholinguists⟩ and linguists are in general agreement that the use of a human language indicates the knowledge of a grammar, even though a good deal of this knowledge is below the conscious level (BC 891). The knowledge of a grammar that children naturally acquire explains their "ultimate ability to create an indeterminable number of meaningful sentences from a finite number of words" (PC 441). While a child may progress from "Mommy milk" to "Mommy, please give me some milk," the apes never moved to this more sophisticated level of expression (TN 20); most longer utterances simply contained repeated signs (GA 299). According to the reports of the Gardners and Patterson, the signs in the apes' sequences occurred in all possible orders (BC

[margin notes: clarify ← unclear √ reference of whatever ← it occurs; Redundant??; Perhaps here there should be a compare/contrast comment focusing on the ape's inability to grasp language?; Again I have trouble figuring out from this sentence the; Isn't this a new point ← demanding a bit more transition?]

point-of view you want to push me toward as a reader.

893); therefore, there is no reason to believe that the apes are acting in accordance with a sense of sign order. Although word order in sign language is less of a "grammatical device" (TN 12) than in spoken language, it is still critical in distinguishing between utterances like "tickle me" and "me tickle" (TN 12-13) and therefore an important key to having a true grasp of the language.

Do avoid passive constructio wherever they occur

Your neutrality (in Language) becomes positively confusing here

As stated by Duane Rumbaugh, a researcher at Georgia State University doing similar work to Terrace's "There is no solid evidence . . . that would indicate that the ape is capable of [uing] language with competence" (LA 57).

Weak: Aren't you using this Qt as a summary your lead in to Qt deemphasi its importan

It's not clear whether the Qt comes from "some" or from Chomsky.

According to many scientists, an apparent inability to use a language's structure denotes an inability to use language itself. Some, like Noam Chomsky, have particularly strong views: "It's about as likely that an ape will prove to have a language ability as that there is an island somewhere with a species of flightless birds waiting for human beings to teach them to fly" (AT 57). As another scientist has expressed it, "the skeptics raise the possibility that the apes have been making monkeys out of their human mentors" (AT 50).

←Is that good? Bad? I can't tell.

←Vague

I'm left at #'s end not esp. clear about what conclusion you want me to draw.

In reworking the above paragraph, the student went beyond a "fix-it" approach to think out how best to solve the logical issues commented on by the teacher. The following revision demonstrates that the student rethought organization and word choice and therefore succeeded in making the material her own.

REVISED III B

Not only did the apes fail to sense the conversational nature of language but, even more importantly, they also seemed to lack any sense of its structure. In natural language, a sentence represents a complete idea through a group of words that have specific grammatical relationships. The relations, unlike the words themselves, cannot be learned individually; they constitute a part of the *grammar* of the language. Linguists generally agree that the use of a human language depends upon the knowledge of its grammar, even though much of the knowledge is below the conscious level (BC 891). The knowledge of a grammar that children naturally acquire explains their "ultimate ability to create an indeterminable number of meaningful sentences from a finite number of words" (PC 441); that is, grammatical knowledge matures with the child, allowing him to progress from the simple imitation of phrases to the construction of sentences he has never heard before. The apes, on the other hand, created sign combinations that varied in order and never increased in complexity, demonstrating their lack of the child's ability to learn to form more complicated utterances and, even more significantly, their lack of the child's sense of language's structure. While a child may progress from "Mommy milk" to "Mommy, please give me some milk," the apes never advanced to this more sophisticated level of expression (TN 20); most long utterances simply contained repeated signs (GA 299). Furthermore, according to the reports of the Gardners and Patterson, the signs in the apes' sequences occurred randomly in utterances like "tickle me" and "me tickle" (TN 12-13). Given this apparent lack of a sense of linguistic order, as well as that of conversational ability and structural complexity, "[t]here is no solid evidence . . . that would indicate that the ape is capable of using [language] with competence" (LA 57).

An extraordinary revision — you go beyond my suggestions to clarify the paragraph's point-of-view and focus. It's so much more clearly expressed than the original; Its Logic (order of material) now works beautifully. You've solved all of the problems I saw in the first paragraph as well as ones I hadn't picked up on: that's real revising! Your judgement about what to edit/rework is excellent

B. DETAILS OF MANUSCRIPT FORM

You have worked hard researching and writing a coherent essay about your subject; therefore, the appearance of your final copy warrants careful attention. Not only should you produce a neatly typed or handwritten paper, but you should also take care to follow details of correct manuscript form, in particular the following items.

1. Title page

Give your paper an interesting title, neither too general nor too cryptic. Remember, it should describe the contents of the paper. Center the title about four inches from the top of the paper. In the lower right quarter of the page, indicate your name, your class, the course title (or titles if the paper was an interdisciplinary project), and the date submitted, thus:

Jane M. Harding
Expository Writing
United States History
December 15, 1999

Jon C. Kim
Senior English
May 31, 2000

2. Outline

Insert the outline immediately after the title page of the finished paper; head it *Contents*. Do not number the pages on which the outline appears.

3. Body of the paper

Leave a margin of one and one-quarter inches at the left and one inch at the right, at the top and at the bottom. Double-space the text and number the pages at the top right in Arabic numerals beginning with page two of the text. Indent quoted passages of more than three lines about an inch from the margin of the text on both left and right, and do not use quotation marks; single-space the indented quotations.

4. Footnotes, endnotes, and parenthetical citations

You may place footnotes at the bottom of the page or use endnotes on a separate sheet at the end of the paper, preceding the bibliography. Many word processing programs allow the writer to place footnotes at the bottom of the page and automatically make the necessary page format adjustments. (See Appendix A for a paper formatted using a computor program for footnotes.) Note that traditional form requires that you single-space footnotes of more than one line, and double-space between footnotes. (See Appendix C.) Whether you choose to use footnotes or endnotes, the citation number should be set in superscript in your text. The first line of the footnote should be indented. All lines after the first in each note must begin at the margin.

Instead of footnotes or endnotes, you may prefer to use parenthetical citations; that is, to document your sources in abbreviated form in parentheses at the end of the sentence, clause, or phrase containing the material which you quote or to which you refer. (See VII B 6 and Appendix B.)

5. Citations in footnote or endnote form
The following are samples of citations (for the footnote or endnote format) which correspond to bibliography entries in Section III C:

1. Printed Works

a. Single Works
Book by one author
[1]Fred J. Cook, Maverick: Fifty Years of Investigative Reporting (New York: G. P. Putnam's Sons, 1984) 138.
Another book by the same author
[2]Fred J. Cook, The Ku Klux Klan: America's Recurring Nightmare (Englewood Cliffs, NJ: J. Messner, 1980) 41.
Book by two authors
[3]Sean Manley and Susan Belcher, O, Those Extraordinary Women! (Philadelphia: Chilton Book Company, 1972) 235.
Book by three or more authors
[4]William L. Masterton et al., Chemical Principles (Philadelphia: Chilton Co., 1972) 372.
Edited work of one author
[5]D. H. Lawrence, Complete Poems, eds. Vivian de Sola Pinto and F. Warren Roberts (New York: Viking Press, 1971) 19.
Translation
[6]Julio Cortazar, Around the Day in Eighty Worlds, trans. Thomas Christensen (San Francisco: North Point Press, 1986) 79.
Corporate author
[7]American Medical Association, The American Medical Association's Handbook of First Aid and Emergency Care (New York: Random House, 1980) 82.

Conference proceedings

[8]Proceedings of the 1985 State Fish and Wildlife Directors Conference. 4-6 June 1985 (Washington, DC: U.S. Department of Commerce, National Marine Fisheries Service, 1986) 72.

Occasional report

[9]Everett Mendelsohn, A Human Reconstruction of Science, a report prepared for a conference on women (Cambridge, MA: Radcliffe Institute, Apr. 1972) 2.

b. Collections

Previously published work in a collection

[10]Paula Fox, "News from the World," Confrontation (Spring, 1975): 78-81, rpt. in Short Shorts: An Anthology of the Shortest Stories (Boston: David R. Godine, 1982) 242.

Work in an edited collection

[11]George Liska, "War and Order," Globalism and Its Critics, ed. William Taubman (Lexington, MA: D. C. Heath and Co., 1973) 42.

Edited collection from which two or more works have been cited

[12]Robert H. Williams, ed., To Live and To Die: When, Why and How (New York: Springer-Verlag, 1973) 24.

One work cited from previously cited edited collection

[13]Gilbert S. Omenn, "Genetic Engineering: Present and Future," in Williams 51.

c. Encyclopedias

Signed article in an encyclopedia

[14]Esmond Wright, "Washington, George," Collier's Encyclopedia 1987 ed.

Unsigned article in an encyclopedia

[15]"Icarus," Encyclopedia Americana 1989 ed.

d. Revisions and Republications
Reprint or facsimile of an earlier edition
[16]Mary Elizabeth Braddon, <u>Lady Audley's Secret</u> (1887; New York: Dover, 1974) 93.
Reprint with new foreword, afterword, or introduction
[17]Clifton Fadiman, afterword, <u>The Red Badge of Courage</u>, by Stephen Crane (New York: Macmillan, 1967) 117.
Edition other than the first
[18]Lawrence Baum, <u>The Supreme Court</u>, 3rd ed. (Washington, DC: Congressional Quarterly, Inc., 1989) 53.

e. Magazines, Journals, and Newspapers
Signed magazine article
[19]Cait Murphy, "Hong Kong: A Culture of Emigration," <u>The Atlantic</u> Apr. 1991: 24.
Unsigned magazine article
[20]"Presidential Commission Cites Improvements in European Airport and Airway Safety," <u>Aviation Week</u> 26 Feb. 1990: 31.
Journal article
[21]Edward Mendelson, "Word Processing: A Guide for the Perplexed," <u>Yale Review</u> 74 (1985): 615.
Unsigned newspaper article showing edition
[22]"Alaska Oil by Land and Sea," <u>New York Times</u> 17 July 1977 nat'l ed.: A4.

f. Government Documents
Printed by Government Printing Office
Report by a government department
[23]United States Bureau of Labor Statistics, <u>A Brief History of the American Labor Movement</u>, 1970 ed. (Washington, DC: GPO, 1970) 120.
Report of hearings
[24]United States, Congress, Senate, Committee on

Government Operations, Subcommittee on Intergovernmental Relations, and Committee on the Judiciary, Subcommittees on Separation of Powers and on Administrative Practice and Procedure, Hearings, 93rd Congress, 1st sess., vol. 1 (Washington, DC: GPO, 1973) 440.

Printed by a private publisher

[25]United States National Advisory Commission on Civil Disorders, Report of the National Advisory Commission on Civil Disorders, New York Times Edition (New York: E. P. Dutton, 1968) 359.

g. Reviews

Book, exhibit or performance

[26]Tom Buckley, "Anyone for War?" rev. of The Long Gray Line by Rick Atkinson, The New York Times Book Review 22 Oct. 1989: 18.

h. Indirect Sources

[27]Marvin Schegel, Ruler of the Reading: The Life of Franklin B. Gowan (Harrisburg: Archives Publishing Co. of Pennsylvania, 1947) 72 as qtd. in Broehl 206.

2. Internet, CD-ROM, and Database Sources

a. Article in a scholarly project

[28]Harold P. Blum, "The Sigmund Freud Archive and the Freud Exhibit at the Library of Congress," Sigmund Freud and the Freud Archives, ed. Robert Salnave, 9 Feb. 1996, The New York Psychoanalytic Inst. and Soc., <http://plaza.interport.net/nypsan/sf a_loc.html> (viewed 26 Apr. 1999).

b. Images in a collection

[29]Antarctic Unit, Tourism Board of Tierra del Fuego, "The Hurley Collection: The British Trans-Antarctic Expedition of 1914/17," Tierra del Fuego: Where America Begins . . . , <http://tierradelfuego.m

l.org/antartida/hurleyeng.htm> (viewed 3 May 1999).

c. An individual picture in a collection
[30] Frank Hurley, Young Emperor Penguins, "The Hurley Collection: The British Trans-Antarctic Expedition of 1914/17," Tierra del Fuego: Where America Begins . . . , Antarctic Unit, Tourism Board of Tierra del Fuego, <http://tierradelfuego.ml.org/ant artida/hurleyeng.htm> (viewed 3 May 1999).

d. A database
[31] Robert Cheetham, ed., "Plant Materials," JGARDEN: Japanese Garden Database, 14 Mar. 1999, <http://pobox.upenn.edu/~cheetham/jgarden /plants.html#tree> (viewed 25 Apr. 1999).

e. Government document
[32] United States, Bureau of the Census, "Poverty 1997: People and Families in Poverty by Selected Characteristics: 1989, 1996, and 1997," Census Bureau Population Topics and Household Economic Topics, 3 Feb. 1999, <http://www.census.gov/hhes/ poverty/poverty97/pv97est1.html> (viewed 21 Apr. 1999).

f. Journal article
[33] Jacquelyn B. James, "The Meanings of Gender," Gender Matters, Spec. issue of Radcliffe Quarterly 3 (1998): 84. <http://www.radcliffe.edu/quarterly/ 199804/meanings_gender.html> (viewed 26 Apr. 1999).

g. Occasional report
[34] Unicef, "Children in War," Introduction, The State of the World's Children: 1996, <http://www.uni cef.org/sowc96/intro.htm> (viewed 8 May 1999).

h. Posting from a discussion list
[35] Ellen Tremper, "Re: Figurative Language

Conveys Character's Uncertainties in <u>Mrs. Dalloway</u>," Online posting, 12 Apr. 1997, VWOOLF, <http://www.utoronto.ca/IVWS/listserv.html> (viewed 13 Apr. 1997).

i. E-mail
[36]Jennett Vosburgh, "Re: WARP," e-mail to Mary Tyler Knowles, 21 Apr. 1999.

j. Radio or television transcript
[37]"Nuclear Espionage?" <u>Online NewsHour with Jim Lehrer</u>, PBS, 30 Apr. 1999, Transcript, <u>Online NewsHour</u>, <http://www.pbs.org/newshour/bb/asia/jan-june99/richardson_4-30.html> (viewed 2 May 1999).

k. An article from a CD-ROM
[38]David Stout, "'Safe Rooms' Urged in Areas Prone to Tornadoes," <u>New York Times</u> 19 Aug. 1998, late ed., East Coast: 18, <u>New York Times Ondisc</u>, CD-ROM, UMI-ProQuest, Sept. 1998.

l. Encyclopedia online
[39]"Burbage, Richard," <u>Encyclopaedia Britannica Online</u>, <http:// www.eb.com> (viewed 26 Apr. 1999).

m. Periodicals via online subscription services (such as Ebsco, Electric Library, InfoTrac, ProQuest Direct, or Lexis-Nexis, etc.)
[40]Aleksa Djilas, "A Profile of Slobodan Milosevic," <u>Foreign Affairs</u> Summer 1993: 81ff., <u>Platinum Periodicals</u>, UMI-ProQuest Direct, Winsor School Lib., Boston, <http://proquest.umi.com/> (viewed 21 Apr. 1999).
[41]Seymour Papert, "Child Psychologist: Jean Piaget : He Found the Secrets of Human Learning and Knowledge Hidden Behind the Cute and Seemingly Illogical Notions of Children," <u>Time</u> 29 Mar. 1999: 100-101, <u>Expanded</u> <u>Academic ASAP</u>,

InfoTrac SearchBank, Winsor School Lib., Boston, <http://www.searchbank.com> (viewed 4 May 1999): 100.

3. Other Media

a. Television or Radio Programs
[42]Private Lives, Public Trust writ. Stephen Schlow, dir. Dimitri Miades, prod. WHDH (a CBS affiliate), Boston, 27 June 1990.

b. Films
[43]Dracula, dir. Todd Browning, with Bela Lugosi, Universal Studios, 1931.

c. Videocassettes or Filmstrips
[44]Hamlet, dir Laurence Olivier, with Laurence Olivier, videocassette, Two Cities Film Ltd., 1948 (155 min.).

d. Lectures and Speeches
[45]David Perkins, "Mrs. Gardner's Circle: T. S. Eliot," Isabella Stewart Gardner Museum, Boston, 2 Nov. 1989.

e. Interviews
Interview conducted by the writer of the paper
[46]David Greuel, Publisher, Wayside Publishing, telephone interview, 24 June 1999.
Interview from a radio or television program
[47]John Dove, "Training for the Boston Marathon for College Credit," All Things Considered, by David Wright, National Public Radio, WGBH, Boston, 15 Apr. 1991.

f. Works of Art
Exhibited painting
[48]Claude Monet, Rouen Cathedral Façade,

Museum of Fine Arts, Boston.
Photograph of a painting
[49] Claude Monet, La Cathédrale de Rouen,
National Gallery of Art, Washington, p. 174 in
Monet by Robert Gordon and Andrew Forge (New
York: Abrams, 1984).

Additional Citation Information:

a. In every case, be sure that the work to which you refer in a footnote or endnote or parenthetical citation is included in your bibliography.

b. The second time you cite a book, state the author but not the title of the work unless you are using two books by the same author, in which case you must give a brief title also.

c. Be aware that citation punctuation differs from that in a works cited or bibliography entry.

d. Throughout the paper, number footnotes or endnotes consecutively using Arabic numerals not followed by periods, parenthesis, or other marks. Put footnote numbers after punctuation at the end of the quotation or other material which requires acknowledgment. Put numbers above line of type both in the text and at the bottom of the page or on a separate sheet at the end of the paper.

e. You may use the following abbreviations and terms in footnote and bibliography entries:

ed.	editor	sc.	scene
eds.	editors	sec.	section
1.	line	trans.	translator
11.	lines	vol.	volume
n.d.	no data (any missing publication information.)	vols.	volumes

f. *Ibid,* meaning "in the same place," and *op cit,* meaning "work already cited," are Latin forms that used to be common. They are not used by contemporary researchers although you may encounter them in your reading.

g. Below are sample citations for a variety of footnotes or endnotes:

First citation of a book (complete)[1]
Same work, different page[2]
First citation of a magazine article[3]
First citation of another book by an author previously cited[4]
Same author, different book previously cited (indicate which book)[5]
Author previously referred to but not immediately before this footnote[6]

[1]Zora Neale Hurston, <u>Dust Tracks on a Road</u> (Philadelphia: J. B. Lippincott Company, 1942) 75.
[2]Hurston 122.
[3]David Joselit, "Public Art & The Public Purse," <u>Art in America</u> July 1990: 145.
[4]Zora Neale Hurston, <u>Their Eyes Were Watching God</u> (Philadelphia: J. B. Lippincott Company, 1937) 87.
[5]Hurston, <u>Dust Tracks</u> 44.
[6]Joselit 143.

6. Citations in parenthetical form

Perhaps the simplest way to document your source of information is to credit the source parenthetically in your text. This format is the one endorsed by *The MLA Handbook*, 5th edition. To create parenthetical references, you should keep them as brief as clarity and accuracy will allow. Insert them at the end of the sentence, clause, or phrase containing the material that is either quoted or referred to. If you include an author's name in the sentence before the citation, you need not include it in the parenthetical page citation that follows. Every author, book, and article to which you refer must be in an alphabetical list of works cited at the end of your essay. Below are sample parenthetical references for various situations:

Citation of a book by a particular author[1]
Same work, different page[2]
Citation of a magazine article[3]
First citation of another book by an author previously cited[4]
Same author, different book from that previously cited[5]
Citation of a periodical from an online subscription service that has an author but no page numbers[6]
Same author and same online subscription service as in[6] but different periodical citation[7]
Citation of an Internet source that has no author and no page numbers[8]
Author named within the sentence before the citation[9]
Author (Hurston) and her text (<u>Dust Tracks</u>) named within the sentence before the citation[10]

[1](Hurston <u>Dust Tracks</u> 75)
[2](Hurston 122)
[3](Joselit "Public Art" 145)
[4](Hurston <u>Their Eyes</u> 87)
[5](Hurston <u>Dust Tracks</u> 44)
[6](Djilas "Poverty" 1997)
[7](Djilas "Tito's Last" 116)
[8]("Dolphins, Porpoises, and Whales—What's the Difference?"<http://www.anca.gov.au/environm/marine/dol dif.htm>)
[9](<u>Dust Tracks</u> 15)
[10](32)

7. Bibliography or List of Works Cited

Include in the final list of works cited only those sources from which you obtained usable material. Refer to section III C for models of correct form and content of entries. Do not number items in the list. Arrange them alphabetically by author (or by title, if a work is unsigned). Do not indent the first line of an entry, but do indent subsequent lines, if any. Single-space each entry, but double-space between entries. Do not number a bibliography or works cited page.

8. Appendix (if necessary)

The appendix is the appropriate place for illustrative or explanatory material that you cannot incorporate into the text. The appendix should have a heading; do not number the pages in the appendix. Place the appendix between the last page of the paper—or after the endnotes (if that is the form you chose)—and the bibliography.

9. Proofreading

As a final step in preparing the research paper, proofread thoroughly and make corrections carefully. Be sure to check for the most common errors: spelling, punctuation, capitalization, inadvertent omissions, and typographical mistakes. Reading the paper aloud will slow down reading speed, thereby enabling you to detect errors more readily. *Proofread your paper more than once*; make corrections neatly.

10. Submitting the Final Paper

Bind the paper neatly in a cover.

APPENDIX A

Field of Greed:

The World Series Scandal of 1919

Susan Pitts
Expository Writing
December 12, 1990

CONTENTS

Thesis Statement: Because fixed games existed long before 1919, because team owner Charles Comiskey paid his players unfairly, and because some of the players who disapproved of the scheme nevertheless did not want to be excluded from the fix, eight members of the Chicago White Sox agreed to lose the World Series of 1919, creating a scandal which threatened the future of baseball until 1921, when baseball's first commissioner, Judge Kenesaw Landis, imposed severe punishments on the eight players in order to convince angry fans that he was purifying the game.

I. Although team owners and baseball officials realized that gambling and fixed games existed long before 1919, they almost always suppressed any investigations into fixed games because proving them was very difficult and because owners and officials knew that fans would not pay to see games they suspected were fixed; because of this unstated policy by owners and officials, many of the participants in the 1919 Series fix believed that, if found out, they would receive little or no punishment.

   A. Even before the Civil War, betting on baseball games was popular, and by the late 1800s, gamblers were bribing players into throwing games.

   B. Hal Chase, a first baseman for the Cincinnati Reds, exemplifies baseball's corruption in the years just prior to the 1919 series.

   C. Because baseball officials and owners did not want the public to discover baseball's corruption, they suppressed any investigations into fixed games; this unstated policy led many of the participants in the 1919 Series fix to believe that they would receive little or no punishment if found out.

II. Although during the few years before the scandal the White Sox drew the largest crowds in all of baseball, team owner Charles Comiskey paid his players the lowest salaries and ignored any attempts by the players to improve their salaries; this cheapness provoked bitterness and resentment among his team members.

    A. Although the White Sox drew the largest crowds in all of baseball from 1917 to 1919, team owner Charles Comiskey paid his players the lowest salaries and was exceedingly cheap concerning team expenses and bonuses.

    B. Although the players often tried to negotiate higher salaries in their contracts, to which they were bound, Comiskey ignored their requests; furthermore, since Comiskey appeared to the fans to be a generous man, the White Sox could not air their grievances successfully in public.

III. While greed caused four of the participants to lose the World Series, the other four participants disapproved of the plan, but because they were told the fix would proceed without them, they decided they did not want to be excluded from the money promised.

    A. First baseman Chick Gandil and shortstop "Swede" Risberg thought up the fix to earn money, and, along with pitcher Ed Cicotte and utility infielder Fred McMullin, proposed it to eager gamblers.

    B. These four conspirators coaxed the other four participants—Buck Weaver, Joe Jackson, Lefty Williams, and Happy Felsch—into losing the World Series by telling them the fix would happen with or without them.

IV. After the public discovered the fixing of the 1919 World Series, fans' distrust of players and their reluctance to go to games greatly diminished baseball's popularity until 1921, when baseball's first commissioner, Judge Kenesaw Landis, imposed severe punishments on the eight players in order to convince the public that he was purifying the game.

A. Baseball fans' dismay at the fixing of the 1919 World Series and their new reluctance to go see games decreased baseball's popularity and threatened its future.

B. In 1921, though a jury acquitted the eight players of conspiracy, the first commissioner of baseball, Judge Kenesaw Landis, after promising to rid baseball of corruption, prohibited the players from playing professional baseball again.

In 1910, President William Howard Taft proclaimed, "The game of baseball . . . is a clean, straight game, and it summons to its presence anybody who enjoys clean, straight athletics."[1] Such was not the case in 1919, however, when eight members of the Chicago White Sox conspired to throw the World Series. The players agreed with prominent gamblers to lose the series for $10,000 each; however, though they succeeded in losing the series, the players never received all of the money promised to them in the fix. Ironically, though rumors had abounded during the series that there was a fix, it was not until September of 1920, a full year later, that the public discovered the rumors were true—a Chicago grand jury which had been investigating gambling in baseball handed down indictments against the eight members of the White Sox. The public was shocked, but what they did not realize at the time was that the Black Sox, as they were dubbed during the scandal, were not the only players involved in corruption, nor were they the first.

Corruption in baseball existed even in its early years. Before the Civil War, betting on baseball games was popular, and by the late 1800s gamblers were bribing players into throwing games. In the early 1800s upper-class men played baseball in private clubs, and many who watched the games, as well as many who played, betted on the games.[2] Baseball was an unorganized sport at this time, and the betting that occurred was minor. In the late 1800s, however, baseball became a fully organized sport, open to all classes, and gambling became more popular and more serious as professional gamblers became involved. Winning a bet was so important to professional gamblers that they often attempted physically to prevent players

---

[1] Harold Seymour, *Baseball: The Golden Years* (New York: Oxford University Press, 1971) 274.

[2] Eliot Asinof, *Eight Men Out* (New York: Holt, Rinehart and Winston, 1963) 10.

from making key plays—a gambler might throw stones at an outfielder trying to catch a crucial fly ball, or he might set off his gun to startle the player.[3] With the increasing popularity of gambling came the fixed game. To secure a successful bet, gamblers realized they could bribe players into losing games with money, whiskey, or women—some gamblers even threatened blackmail or violence.[4] Not all ballplayers were willing to cooperate with the gamblers, however; therefore, gamblers targeted with their bribes older players (near the end of their careers), poorly paid players, and players with personal problems.[5] Sometimes though, gamblers could bribe whole teams into throwing games. In the 1860s the Troy (New York) Haymakers were notorious for throwing games.[6] One might think fixed games would decrease baseball's popularity, but teams who fixed games took turns losing to each other so that they would not arouse public suspicion.[7] Thus, even in its early years, gambling and fixed games were prevalent in baseball.

Hal Chase, a first baseman for the Cincinnati Reds, exemplifies baseball's corruption in the years just prior to the 1919 World Series. Chase was an excellent fielder and hitter who often arranged with gamblers to fix games. For years, Chase had the ability to throw games without arousing suspicion. If a batter hit a key ground ball to him, Chase would stop it correctly, but then he would throw the ball to first base just before the pitcher could catch it. Thus, the pitcher looked bad, and no one suspected Chase of throwing the game.[8] During a game in 1917, Chase attempted to bribe a relief pitcher into losing a tied

---

[3] Harold Seymour, *Baseball: The Early Years* (New York: Oxford University Press, 1960) 53.

[4] Asinof 13.

[5] Asinof 13.

[6] Seymour, *The Early Years* 53.

[7] Seymour, *The Early Years* 54.

game. The pitcher refused but lost the game anyway, and Chase, thinking the pitcher lost purposely, gave him fifty dollars. The pitcher told his manager, who informed the National League President. A hearing was held for Chase, but he was acquitted because of insufficient evidence. Though Chase's manager, an honest man, refused to let Chase stay on his team, the New York Giants signed him, and Chase remained in baseball and continued to throw games. Though Chase exemplifies the corruption of players, he is proof of the deviation of team owners as well.

Because officials and team owners did not want the public to discover baseball's corruption, they suppressed any investigations into fixed games; this unstated policy led many of the participants in the 1919 Series fix to believe they would receive little or no punishment if found out. Team owners realized that satisfactory attendance at their games depended on the belief the games were completely honest; therefore, owners denied the existence of betting on baseball and had never punished any corrupt players prior to 1919.[9] It is possible that the players involved in the 1919 Series scandal did not believe team owners would punish them for their actions either.[10] Such beliefs may have stemmed from the Hal Chase incident. In 1920, journalist Hugh Fullerton wrote:

> The Chase case gave many players the idea they could play dishonestly and not be discovered . . . the club owners have always adhered to the policy of secrecy and have whitewashed every scandal and charge of crooked work on the grounds that it was for the good of the game. Their policy encour-

---

[8] Hugh Fullerton, "Baseball on Trial," *The New Republic* 20 Oct. 1920: 184.

[9] Donald Gropman, *Say It Ain't So Joe!* (Boston: Little, Brown and Co., 1979) 164.

[10] Glenn Dickey, *The History of the World Series Since 1903* (New York: Stein and Day Pub., 1984) 63.

aged crooked ball players.[11]

Ed Cicotte, one of the White Sox fix participants, said during the trial that he assumed owners would protect him from punishment because he had seen how they protected other corrupt players in the past.[12] Thus, owners' attitudes influenced the White Sox in agreeing to lose the World Series.

Charles Comiskey was an owner whose attitudes about money seemed designed to foster corruption on his team. Although the White Sox drew the largest crowds in all baseball from 1917 to 1919, team owner Charles Comiskey paid his players the lowest salaries and was exceedingly cheap about team expenses and bonuses. Comiskey paid $65,000 to buy Joe Jackson from Cleveland, yet Jackson's salary with the White Sox was only $6,000 per year.[13] Jackson, one of the best players in baseball at this time, was the highest-paid player on the White Sox; however, the highest salary on the Cincinnati Reds team was $10,000 per year, the second highest $9,000, and the third highest $8,000.[14] In comparison with their achievements on the field, the Sox salaries were extremely low. Ed Cicotte was a fourteen-year veteran pitcher in 1919. He won twenty-eight games in 1917 (in comparison, 1990's highest game-winning pitcher won twenty-four games) but in 1919 received less than $6,000 per year.[15] During the 1919 season Comiskey promised Cicotte a $10,000 bonus if he won thirty games, but after Cicotte won twenty-nine games, Comiskey refused to let him pitch until the playoffs (when winning games are no longer included in a pitcher's record). Comiskey also

---

[11] Fullerton 184.

[12] Gropman 183.

[13] Dickey 63.

[14] Dickey 63.

[15] Asinof 16.

promised the whole team a bonus if they won the 1917 pennant. When they did, their bonus was a case of champagne. [16] Comiskey was parsimonious in other areas, too. He gave his players a $3 per day meal allowance; all other teams received a minimum of $4 per day. [17] What did Comiskey do with all of his money? In 1909, Comiskey spent $500,000 rebuilding his ballpark. [18] Not only did he dedicate this park to the people of Chicago, but he also let them use the park for special events—for free. [19] Thus, to the public, Comiskey seemed a generous person.

Although the players often tried to negotiate higher salaries in their contracts, to which they were bound, Comiskey ignored their requests; furthermore, since Comiskey appeared to the fans to be a generous person, the White Sox could not air their grievances successfully in public. One of the White Sox's problems was the Reserve Clause, found in every major league player's contract. The clause stated that if a player refused to accept the terms offered to him by the owner, no other club could hire him. [20] Thus, a player could not really negotiate a salary at all—he either accepted the money offered him by the owner, or he did not play for that year. In 1918, Comiskey once again refused to discuss salary changes, and the White Sox threatened to strike. [21] In order to prevent controversy, however, their manager, "Kid" Gleason, dissuaded them even though he agreed with his team's reasons for wanting to strike. [22] The White Sox could not complain openly about Comiskey, for who would believe Comiskey was cheap when he had recently dedicated his

---

[16] Asinof 22.

[17] Asinof 21.

[18] Asinof 51.

[19] Asinof 51.

[20] Asinof 21.

[21] Asinof 16.

[22] Asinof 16.

new ballpark to the people of Chicago? Thus, the White Sox, the most talented team in baseball, played year after year for the stingiest man in baseball, until the World Series scandal of 1919.

In spite of gamblers' history of bribing players, it was the players themselves who first proposed the fix to the gamblers. First baseman Chick Gandil and shortstop "Swede" Risberg thought up the plan to earn money, and, along with pitcher Ed Cicotte and utility infielder Fred McMullin, proposed it to eager gamblers. During the trial Ed Cicotte stated, "Before Gandil became a ball player, he was mixed up with gamblers . . That's where he got the idea to put the fix on the World Series."[23] Long after the trial, Gandil himself admitted it was he who was the first to approach gamblers with his plan.[24] Gandil discussed his idea with Risberg, and the two decided they needed eight players to agree to throw the series. McMullin overheard the discussion and wanted to be included.[25] Gandil then proposed the fix to Cicotte, who refused but later agreed. "I was thinking of my wife and kids and how I needed the money," he later stated in his confession.[26] Indeed, Cicotte needed the money to pay off a large mortgage on his Michigan farm;[27] however, after agreeing to participate in the fix, he became greedy. The original agreement between these four men and a gambler named Joseph Sullivan stated that the players would receive $80,000 ($10,000 each) if they could guarantee that eight players would participate in throwing the series. After the players closed this deal with Sullivan, Cicotte and Gandil

---

[23] Joe Reichler, *The World Series: 76th Anniversary Edition* (New York: Simon and Schuster, 1979) 147.

[24] Seymour, *The Golden Years* 332.

[25] Asinof 17.

[26] "White Sox Players Are All Acquitted by Chicago Jury." *New York Times* 3 Aug. 1921: 2.

[27] Asinof 16-17.

offered the same proposition to another gambler, Arnold Rothstein. Instead of receiving $80,000, however, the players demanded $100,000,[28] Rothstein agreed, and all that was left to do was to convince four more players to participate.

These four conspirators coaxed the other four participants—"Happy" Felsch, "Lefty" Williams, "Shoeless" Joe Jackson, and "Buck" Weaver—into losing the World Series by telling them the fix would happen with or without them. During the players' trial, Happy Felsch confessed:

> I didn't want to get in on the deal at first. . . . But when they let me in on the idea, too many men were involved. I didn't like to be a squealer and I knew that if I stayed out of the deal and said nothing they would go ahead without me and I'd be that much money out without accomplishing anything.[29]

Lefty Williams gave the same reason as Felsch for participating in the fix. Gandil presented the situation clearly to Williams: if he cooperated, he'd earn $10,000; if he didn't, he would receive nothing, and the team would lose the series anyway. Although both Jackson and Weaver agreed to throw the series for the same reasons as Felsch and Williams, their performances in the World Series do not reflect their decisions to participate. Jackson, for example, had a .375 average for the World Series, the highest on his team.[30] Gandil offered Jackson $10,000 to participate, and then $20,000.[31] Jackson refused both times. After Gandil

---

[28] Asinof 27.

[29] Asinof 190.

[30] John Durant, *Highlights of the World Series* (New York: Hastings House Pub., 1973) 83.

[31] Gropman 163.

nagged him continuously, however, Jackson finally agreed to the proposition. It is evident, however, that Jackson was not an active participant. He neither attended meetings with gamblers nor purposely attempted to lose any of the games.[32] Nevertheless, Jackson received $5,000 from the gamblers.[33] Buck Weaver also had an excellent Series, batting .324[34] and committing no errors,[35] but he received no money from the gamblers.[36] Though he had at first agreed to the fix and had attended two meetings with the gamblers, Weaver changed his mind, openly expressed his disapproval of the fix and defied the gamblers by playing to his potential. Author Eliot Asinof wrote about Weaver: "There was no bitterness, no hatred, no frustration powerful enough to corrupt his love for baseball!"[37] Though Buck Weaver played his best and received nothing in the fix, he eventually received the same severe punishment given to the other seven players by the commissioner.

After the Series the eight players continued playing for the White Sox. Late in the season of 1920, however, a grand jury handed down indictments against them; thus the public learned of the scandal. Baseball fans' dismay at the fixing of the 1919 World Series and their new reluctance to go see games greatly diminished baseball's popularity and threatened its future. Fans had always put great faith in baseball players. Now the World Series scandal destroyed this confidence.[38] In 1921, a writer in *The Nation* stated:

---

[32] Asinof 253.

[33] Dickey 68.

[34] Durant 83.

[35] Seymour, *The Golden Years* 333.

[36] Dickey 68.

[37] Asinof 63.

[38] Durant 55.

We do not trust cashiers half so much, or diplo-
mats, or policeman or physicians, as we trust an
outfielder or a shortstop. . . . The one thing he is
not called is a sneak or a traitor. The man at bat is
supposed to be doing his best. . . . To find out that
famous players have been corrupted is more than
to lose faith in them personally; it is to begin to
doubt the whole system. . . .[39]

Fans did not blame only the eight players involved in the
fix. They reasoned that if there was corruption on one
team, there was probably corruption on other teams as
well.[40] Fans, therefore, no longer wanted to pay to see
games they suspected were fixed, and their grievances did
not end with the players. Many fans complained about the
National Commission, a group of three men who governed
baseball prior to 1921.[41] Although both fans and baseball
officials had felt that the National Commission was weak,
they now blamed it for not being able to protect the players from gamblers.[42] They also claimed that if the
National Commission had been an organized, powerful
body, officials would have known of the scandal earlier,
and they would have been able to impose punishments
faster.[43] Thus, because fans were angry at both the players and the governing body of the game, team owners
decided they needed a new system of power in baseball.

Baseball's new system of government consisted of a
commissioner. The appointment of baseball's first commissioner is attributed to a prominent businessman named

---

[39] "The Baseball Scandal," *The Nation* 13 Oct. 1920: 395, as
quoted in Durant 55.

[40] "Scandal" 396.

[41] Asinof 200.

[42] Asinof 200.

[43] Asinof 200.

Albert Lasker. Lasker believed club owners were not capable of ruling baseball.[44] Instead, he proposed that, because baseball belonged to the public, the owners should chose a man financially detached from baseball to govern it.[45] This commissioner should have the power to impose fines on both players and owners.[46] Although Lasker proposed his plan before the World Series scandal, he received little support for it until 1921, when owners finally realized the need for change.[47] In 1921, the owners chose Kenesaw Mountain Landis, a prominent judge, for their first commissioner. Coincidentally, in the same year the eight players were brought to trial for conspiracy. Even before the trial, Landis had sworn, "there [was] no chance for any [of the eight players] to creep back into baseball."[48] Landis fulfilled his promise. A few months later, though a jury acquitted the players, Landis issued this statement:

> Regardless of the verdict of juries, no player who throws a ball game, no player that undertakes or promises to throw a ball game, no player that sits in conference with a bunch of crooked players and gamblers, where the ways and means of throwing a game are discussed and does not promptly tell his club about it, will ever play professional baseball again![49]

After imposing this punishment, Landis was regarded as a hero who cleaned up baseball.[50] Landis remained adamant in his decision for punishment. Five months

---

[44] Seymour, *The Golden Years* 311.

[45] Seymour, *The Golden Years* 312.

[46] Seymour, *The Golden Years* 312.

[47] Seymour, *The Golden Years* 312.

[48] Seymour, *The Golden Years* 323.

[49] Gropman 201.

[50] Seymour, *The Golden Years* 339.

after the trial, Buck Weaver asked Landis for reinstatement. Landis' reply (which he issued to the press, not Weaver) stated "birds of a feather flock together. Men associating with gamblers and crooks [can] expect no leniency."[51] Though a jury had acquitted the eight players of conspiracy, baseball's first commissioner, after promising to rid baseball of corruption,[52] prohibited the players from playing baseball ever again.

Thus, because fixed games existed long before 1919, because team owner Charles Comiskey paid his players unfairly, and because some of the players who disapproved of the scheme, nevertheless, did not want to be excluded from it, eight members of the Chicago White Sox agreed to lose the World Series of 1919. This scandal threatened the future of baseball until 1921, when baseball's first commissioner, Judge Landis, imposed severe punishments on the eight players in an effort to convince angry fans that he was purifying the game. In a way, the scandal of 1919 was inevitable because of the prevalence of corruption and the weakness of baseball's officials. Fortunately, Landis became involved in the situation. Some people argue that Landis' punishments, particularly of Weaver and Jackson, were too harsh. But Landis was correct. Had he allowed Jackson and Weaver to continue playing, he probably would not have convinced fans that baseball was once again clean. Landis needed to prove that he would not allow any player even remotely associated with corruption to stay in the game. Landis also sent the message to other players that he would tolerate no further corruption. Thus, President Taft was correct in stating baseball was a "clean, straight game." It never had been before, but because Landis intervened, he saved the game from self-destructing.

---

[51] Seymour, *The Golden Years* 339.

[52] Asinof 280.

BIBLIOGRAPHY*

Asinof, Eliot. *Eight Men Out*. New York: Holt, Rinehart and Winston, 1963.

"The Baseball Scandal." *The Nation* 13 Oct. 1920: 395-396.

Dickey, Glenn. *The History of the World Series Since 1903*. New York: Stein and Day Pub., 1984.

Durant, John. *Highlights of the World Series*. New York: Hastings House Pub., 1984.

Fullerton, Hugh. "Baseball on Trial." *The New Republic* 20 Oct. 1920: 183-184.

Gropman, Donald. *Say It Ain't So Joe!* Boston: Little, Brown and Co., 1979.

Reichler, Joe. *The World Series 76th Anniversary Edition*. New York: Simon and Schuster, 1979.

Seymour, Harold. *Baseball: The Early Years*. New York: Oxford University Press, 1960.

Seymour, Harold. *Baseball: The Golden Years*. New York: Oxford University Press, 1971.

"White Sox Players Are All Acquitted By a Chicago Jury." *New York Times* 3 Aug. 1921: 2.

---

* The writer chose to indicate all book and magazine titles in italics (as a printer would) instead of underlining them.

APPENDIX B

Black Holes: Journey Toward the Pull

Silvia F. Spring
Expository Writing
June 16, 1999

Contents

Thesis Statement: Since the mathematical theory of black holes first arose in 1796, black holes have fascinated the scientific world, inspiring physicists and astrophysicists to observe their effects on their surroundings and come to conclusions about their structure.

I. Using the physics of gravity, mathematicians theorized that there could possibly be a star so massive that the acceleration of its gravity could exceed the escape velocity of light.

    A. The gravitational force that holds people to the surface of the earth is the same force that attracts all matter in the universe to all other matter.

    B. Using Newtonian ideas about gravity, scientists theorized that there could be a star with a gravitational attraction strong enough to recapture all of its own light.

II. With these mathematical theories in mind, scientists were able to explain their observations of distorted rotating stars and radiation by inferring the existence of black holes.

    A. Because of their strong gravitational pull, black holes suck in matter from stars around them and cause stars to rotate around them.

    B. Researchers are able to detect the jets' emissions and predict the location of the black hole when a black hole releases jets of radiation from its poles as it pulls in matter.

III. From observing how black holes affect stars around them, researchers have been able to determine how black holes are able to distort the matter and light that fall into them.

    A. Black holes exert their strong gravitational pull in the form of tidal forces which stretch and distort matter as it enters the black hole.

B. The pull that tidal forces exert also stretches light waves, capturing them and distorting the light going into the black hole.

IV. Because we are able to observe and measure the effects black holes have on other matter, researchers are now able to define the properties of their structure.

A. The infinitely small point at which all of the black hole's matter lies is called a singularity.

B. Surrounding this point of singularity is the event horizon, which acts as a one-way membrane though which light and matter can enter but never exit.

I became possessed with the keenest curiosity
about the whirl itself. I positively felt a
wish to explore its depths, even at the
sacrifice I was going to make; and
my principal grief was that I
should never be able to
tell my old companions
onshore about the
mysteries I
should

s

e

e

-Edgar Allan Poe
"A Descent into the Maelstrom,"
1840

For centuries, people have sought to answer the questions of where our universe comes from, what the stars and planets are made of, and why they rotate and revolve as they do. As technology has progressed, we have been able to look deeper into space and answer more of these questions from a distance. Because earth is so distant from galaxies and the stars outside of our solar system, the job of an astronomer today is still centered around observation, and researchers continue to rely on what they see through telescopes as evidence of what the seemingly infinite universe in which we live is made. While most other types of scientists find something, define it, then ask how it works, astronomers, astrophysicists and cosmologists must record how something is working and moving in space, and then ask what it is. This technique proved most useful in the discovery of black holes, as black holes are impossible to see but are responsible for much of the movement in our universe. The theory of black holes stood for decades as a mathematical theory until researchers could find no other answer to the question of why matter was moving as it was within the cosmos. The actual existence of black holes was a matter of controversy as recently as three years ago, but since then, with their new technology, astronomers have accumulated a large amount of new evidence supporting the idea that black holes not only exist in our galaxy, but also are a commonplace in almost every galaxy. Since the mathematical theory of black holes first arose in 1796, they have fascinated the scientific world, inspiring physicists and astrophysicists to observe their effects on their surroundings and come to conclusions about their structure.

Before astronomers even had the capability to look beyond the realm of our galaxy, mathematicians used the physics of gravity to theorize that there could possibly be a star so massive that the acceleration of its gravity could exceed the escape velocity of light. The gravitational force that holds people to the surface of the earth is the same force that attracts all matter to all other matter. The force of gravity pulls all objects to the earth with a force of about ten newtons for every kilogram of mass, which means that if you dropped a ball from any height, its downward speed would increase at a rate of ten meters per second each second. Newton's law of universal gravitation states that every two particles of matter in the universe attract each other with a force that depends on their masses and the distance between them (Fix 83). Therefore, if the earth were the same size but more massive, it would pull with a greater force, and, if it were less massive, it would pull with a weaker force. Theoretically, if the earth were massive enough, its gravity would be so strong that humans would be flattened and light would not be able to escape, thus making it a black hole. Because all the planets and matter in the universe obey the same law of gravity, they all reciprocally respond to each other's masses by attracting and by being attracted. The gravitational force exerted by stars like our sun, many times greater than the gravitational force felt on earth, is responsible for our revolving around the sun, and for all revolving matter in our universe. Understanding how gravity works on our own planet helped researchers discover how gravity affects stars and black holes.

Using Newtonian ideas about gravity, French scientist Pierre Simon Laplace theorized in 1796 that there could be a star with a gravitational attraction strong enough to recapture all of its own light. Laplace knew that the gravity of the earth on the earth's surface causes objects to accelerate at a rate of ten meters per second, so he set out to explore how the force of gravity could affect the speed of light (Boslough 61). Yet it wasn't until 1916 that German physicist Karl Schwarzschild introduced the modern view of black holes by completing Einstein's equations and discovering the escape velocity equation (Kaler 450-1). The escape velocity equation dictates how fast objects must travel to escape the pull of gravity. If the escape velocity exceeds the speed of light, nothing, not even light, can escape. Schwarzschild was the first to calculate the mass and volume needed to cause a gravitational pull so strong that no light could escape. A large mass within a small volume creates the strongest gravitational pull, and so, more important than the mass of an object is its density. Until Schwarzschild, most physicists believed that the most dense thing in the universe was the neutron star, which is a small burnt out star only one or two times the mass of our sun. Though its density is great, light can escape it. Theorists predicted that there must be some limit to the density of a neutron star and if that limit were passed, the star would no longer be able to radiate light. Though Laplace, Schwarzschild, and many others theorized about the mathematical idea of black holes, black holes remained just a theory until 1939 when physicists Oppenheimer and Snyder finally took seriously the possibility that stars a few times more dense than our sun might collapse to an infinitely small point at the end of their lives and become black holes, and the two were the first to begin searching for observational evidence. Because so much of the mathematical work had been completed prior to the search for evidence, researchers knew what evidence would support the theory of black holes.

With these mathematical theories in mind, scientists were able to explain their observations of distorted rotating stars and detected x-ray radiation by inferring the existence of black holes. Though black holes radiate no energy, researchers can find them by their effects on their surroundings. Researchers noted that there were stars rotating around unidentifiable gravitational sources. Just as the earth rotates around the sun because of gravitational pull, many stars in the universe were then predicted and are now thought to rotate around black holes. Yet the image seen from earth appears as a star rotating around dark empty space. By observing the orbit of the visible neighbor star around the 'invisible matter,' scientists are able to calculate the mass of what the stars are spinning around (Pickover 6) and to determine whether it is more massive than three times the mass of the sun, which would make it a possible black hole. In 1995, the Very Long Baseline Array (VBLA) peered into galaxy NGC 4258 and measured the whirling motion of a gas clocked at 900 km per second orbiting the galactic core and concluded that the core had a density of 100 million suns per cubic light year, thereby exceeding the density of any galactic center ever measured (Pickover 6) and increasing the probability of the existence of a black hole at its center. Astronomers reason that an unseen source with a high mass points directly to black holes: "If a compact object shows a mass of, say, eight suns then we infer the presence of a black hole because we do not believe that neutron stars this massive can exist . . ." (Charles and Wagner). Researchers have concluded that if an object is more massive than the mass limit of a neutron star, its density will increase without limit and its gravity will be enough to hold in all of its light. The star is then defined as a black hole.

Another observation that is indicative of black holes is detected radiation. When a black hole releases jets of radiation from its poles as it pulls in matter, researchers are able to detect the jets' emissions and to infer the existence and location of the black hole. While scanning the heavens for light radiation, researchers stumbled across a number of x-ray sources coming seemingly from nowhere. They concluded that the gas must be coming from the remains of a star that was being ripped apart by some gravitational force. Researchers have concluded that, as matter falls into a black hole, "[g]as around a black hole collects into a

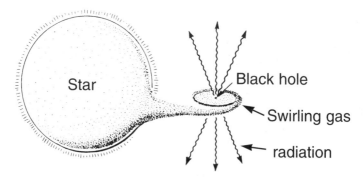

Here a black hole consumes a star, swirling its matter
into a disc and releasing x-rays from its poles (Gribbin 111)

disc because of its large angular momentum . . . which prevent[s] the gas from falling into a black hole, inducing it to rotate instead" (Bisnovatyi-Kogan). The gravity of the black hole swings the gas at such an incredibly fast speed that much of the gas is suspended and kept from falling inward. Energy from the gas which does fall in is converted into x-rays and heat that can travel millions of light years to be detected here on earth. Some energy which enters the hole can actually come out again. In 1969, Roger Penrose suggested ". . . that energy could be extracted from a black hole—if it were rotating. This idea was called super radiance and suggested that certain types of waves in the vicinity of a black hole would be amplified and thrown off—rather than absorbed—by the black hole" (Boslough 71). What Penrose theorized was that the energy of the black hole's rotation could, in special circumstances, be carried away by particles which passed nearby. X-ray emission from galaxies such as Cygnus X-1 is a prime clue that a black hole is present.

From observing how black holes affect stars around them, researchers have been able to determine how the gravity of black holes distorts the matter and light that fall into them. Black holes exert their strong gravitational pull in the form of tidal forces that stretch and deform matter as it enters the black hole. As an object begins to rotate closer and closer to a black hole, the tidal forces exert a greater pull on the side of the matter closer to the black hole than on the far side of it, thereby creating a stretching effect until the matter is ripped apart. "J. P. Luminet suggests that at the [edge of a black hole] the stretching effect would be the same as if you were hanging from the girder of the Eiffel Tower with the entire population of Paris suspended at your knees" (Pickover 78). The stretching effect pulls on bigger things until they rip apart and then does the same to their parts, working its way down to the molecular and atomic levels until the infalling object is completely shredded into microscopic bits.

The pull that tidal forces exert also stretches light waves, capturing them and distorting the light going into the black hole. Because light travels in waves, it is not affected the same way gas and matter are. While light waves can be stretched or crushed, they cannot be spun around into a disc. As light travels into a black hole, photons, which make up the light wave, get caught outside of the hole in the place where their velocity is barely sufficient to allow them to withstand the hole's gravity. Because they can't escape and don't fall in, the photons produce the image that anything falling toward the hole and giving off light is trapped where the photons sit. This means that if a person were to fall into a black hole, someone watching would think that the person had stopped just outside the hole when, in actuality, the person continued to fall. As the light waves that do continue to fall trav-

Light Ray — Your Eye

Event Horizon

Black Hole

The black hole squeezes the light waves together into a bright circular disk above your head (Pickkover 26)

el into the back hole, they are pulled together into a tight circle to fit inside the hole, like rushing water going down a bath tub drain. If someone were to stand inside a black hole, he would see an image of the universe crushed into a tight circle. The black hole's gravity produces this gravitational lens that squeezes his view of the universe into a bright circular disk above his head in order to fit all of the light into its center (Pickover 12). Because black holes have the power to distort light, which is the only kind of message that can travel through space, the resulting visual effects would be misleading.

Researchers' ability to observe and measure the effects black holes have on matter enabled them to define the properties of their structure. The infinitely small point at which all of the black hole's matter lies is called a *singularity*. Between 1965 and 1970 Roger Penrose and Stephen Hawking proved that there must be a singularity of infinite density and spacetime curvature within all black holes. Inside the center of a black hole, "a black hole's mass is crammed within a singularity which essentially has a volume of zero" (Pickover 52). Hawking noted that at a singularity many, if not all, of the laws of science and physics break down. Because these singularities are places where science fails, their presence causes serious problems for many laws of physics such as energy conservation (Chaisson and McMillan) because all energy that is pulled into a singularity seems to disappear. A black hole is essentially its singularity because this is where the mass lies and where all its gravitational force comes from.

Surrounding this point of singularity is the event horizon, which acts as a one way membrane though which light and matter can enter but never exit. If you were to envision a black hole as a sphere, the black hole's surface would be the event horizon. Behind this horizon, the inward pull of gravity is so overwhelming that no information about the black hole's interior can escape to the outside universe. It separates light rays that are trapped from those that can move away from it; however, some light rays that are moving away at a given instant of time may find themselves trapped later if more matter or energy falls into the black hole, increasing its gravitational pull and the radius of its event horizon.Though there is no kind of visible bound-

Event Horizon

Singularity

Artistic representation of a black hole (Pickover 46)

ary in space marking out the edges of this horizon, astronomers use it as a boundary beyond which anything entering will most certainly be pulled to the singularity. As with the singularity, scientists know nothing about the conditions inside of the event horizon, nor do our laws of physics apply there (Kaler 451). Some physicists think that "[a]t the event horizon itself, the curvature of space is so great that space folds over on itself, causing objects within it to become trapped and disappear" (Chaisson and McMillan 475). The truth is nobody really knows what lies inside because within the event horizon, no light or matter of any kind can escape to reflect what the inside is made of or looks like.

Because it is so difficult to imagine what infinite spacetime curvature really is and because all known physics breaks down at the singularity, many physicists are letting their imaginations supersede their observations and are building an enormous number of new theories on speculation. Even though black holes are invisible and are not yet fully understood, physicists nonetheless use them to explain everything from the creation of galaxies and quasars to the ultimate fate of the universe. Already, physicists are coming up with ideas of 'white holes,' which would have no gravity, and, in contrast with black holes, would spit out matter, but the probability of their existence is very slim. Cosmologist Kip Thorne and his graduate student Michael Morris went so far as to develop and publish a theoretical scheme for interstellar and intrastellar universal travel in *The American Journal of Physics*, in which they suggest the theoretical possibility for worm holes that could bridge the universe (Pickover 127). The concept of infinite mass and spacetime curvature in zero volume at the singularity opens the door to many options such as the reality of time travel and interstellar gateways. With so much new information and so much still unknown, it is sometimes hard to keep in mind that it is very possible that the infinitely small point of singularity may be just an infinitely small point in space. However, skeptics should keep in mind that just under a decade ago black holes were also just mathematical theories and unsolved equations.

WORKS CITED

Andersen, Michael Cramer. "Curvature and Light Cones." Geometry Around Black Holes. 18 June 1997. Relativistic Computer Dynamics and Visualization Course. <http://www.astro.ku.dk/~cramer/RelViz/> (Viewed 1 June 1999).

- - -. "General Relativity and Black Holes." Geometry Around Black Holes. 18 June 1997. Relativistic Computer Dynamics and Visualization Course. <http://www.astro.ku.dk/~cramer/RelViz/> (Viewed 1 June 1999).

- - -. "Kerr's Rotating Black Holes." Geometry Around

Black Holes. 18 June 1997. Relativistic Computer
Dynamics and Visualization Course.
<http://www.astro.ku.dk/~cramer/RelViz/> (Viewed 1
June 1999).

"Ask Astro." Astronomy Apr. 1998. Platinum Periodicals.
UMI-ProQuest Direct. Winsor School Lib., Boston.
<http://proquest.umi.com/> (Viewed 20 Apr. 1999).

Bisnovatyi-Kogan, G.S. "At the Border of Eternity."
Science 27 Feb. 1998. Platinum Periodicals. UMI-
ProQuest Direct. Winsor School Lib., Boston.
<http://proquest.umi.com/> (Viewed 22 Apr. 1999).

Boslough, John. Stephen Hawking's Universe. New York:
Morrow, 1985.

Bunn, Ted. "Black Holes FAQ." A Wormhole in the
Cosmos. 8 May 1998.
<http://www.intothecosmos.com> (Viewed 16 June
1999).
Chaisson, Eric and Steve McMillan. Astronomy Today.
New Jersey: Prentice, 1997.

Charles, Philip A. and Mark R. Wagner. "Black Holes in
Binary Stars: Weighing the Evidence." Sky and
Telescope May 1996. Platinum Periodicals. UMI-
ProQuest Direct. Winsor School Lib., Boston.
<http://proquest.umi.com/> (Viewed 20 Apr. 1999).

"Event Horizon Heralded." Sky and Telescope Apr. 1997.
Platinum Periodicals. UMI-ProQuest Direct. Winsor
School Lib., Boston. <http://proquest.umi.com/>
(Viewed 23 Apr. 1999).

Fix, John D. Astronomy: Journey to the Cosmic Frontier.
Dubuque, IA: Brown, 1995.

"Fueling a Black Hole's Jets." Sky and Telescope Apr.

1998. <u>Platinum Periodicals</u>. UMI-ProQuest Direct. Winsor School Lib., Boston. <http://proquest.umi.com/> (Viewed 27 Apr. 1999).

Gribbin, John. <u>Unveiling The Edge of Time: Black Holes, White Holes, Wormholes</u>. New York: Harmony, 1992.

Kaler, James B. <u>Astronomy!</u> New York: HarperCollins, 1994.

Pickover, Clifford A. <u>Black Holes: A Traveler's Guide</u>. New York: Wiley, 1996.

Sawyer, Kathy. "Evidence of Escape From a Black Hole's Pull; Astronomers Find a Cosmic Version of Old Faithful 40,000 Light-Years From Earth." <u>Washington Post</u> 8 Jan. 1998. <u>Platinum Periodicals</u>. UMI-ProQuest Direct. Winsor School Lib., Boston. <http://proquest.umi.com/> (Viewed 20 Apr. 1999).

- - -. "Score Another One for Einstein; X-ray Data Indicate Dense, Spinning Objects Do Drag Space and Time." <u>The Washington Post</u> 7 Nov. 1997. <u>Platinum Periodicals</u>. UMI-ProQuest Direct. Winsor School Lib., Boston. <http://proquest.umi.com/> (Viewed 20 Apr. 1999).

"Seeing the Edges of Black Holes." <u>Astronomy</u> May 1997. <u>Platinum Periodicals</u>. UMI-ProQuest Direct. Winsor School Lib., Boston. <http://proquest.umi.com/> (Viewed 27 Apr. 1999).

Smoot, George and Keav Davidson. <u>Wrinkles in Time</u>. New York: Morrow, 1993.

Wilford, John Noble. "Escaping Doom in a Black Hole." <u>Union Tribune</u> 11 Feb 1998. <u>Platinum Periodicals</u>. UMI-ProQuest Direct. Winsor School Lib., Boston. <http://proquest.umi.com/> (Viewed 24 Apr. 1999).

APPENDIX C

The Golden Age of Monasticism?: A.D. 547-1536

Louisa Anne Burnham
Expository Writing
December 12, 1980

CONTENTS

Thesis Statement: Although the institution of monasticism contributed greatly to medieval life through a distribution of charity and the atmosphere of learning and culture that surrounded it, the daily life of the individual monastery was often rendered corrupt by the frequent bypassing, by both the abbots and the monastic community in general, of the traditions and the way of life established by St. Benedict's Rule.

I. Medieval society benefited from the presence of the monasteries because of the charity and hospitality they distributed to the poor and travelers, and because of the many intellectual and cultural contributions they had to offer.

    A. According to monastic tradition, the monks offered charity by means of guest houses and meals to the poor and to travelers, thus benefiting much of the population.

    B. The monasteries were also great centers for intellectual and cultural growth: the monks were among the most educated people in the world, and they initiated a great many of the important advances in literature, architecture, and music.

II. The abbot, the most important member of any monastic community, was gradually forced to relinquish his role as the father of the community; in order to fulfill his obligations as a feudal lord, he could no longer live as an ordinary monk nor set a good example to his fellow monks.

    A. As his monastery began to possess more and more land and as his feudal and administrative responsibilities increased, the medieval abbot found himself to be increasingly estranged from the ordinary life of his abbey.

B. Since the abbot was the very "pivot on which the life of the monastery turned," if he were a strong, spiritual man, the monastery would follow suit, but, conversely, if he were weak, or highly secular, the monks could do (and did) as they pleased.

III. The high ideals set forth in the monastic Rules were often rendered corrupt by not being followed word for word and were sometimes abandoned almost entirely.

A. Since they followed the secular example set by the abbots, it was a common sight to see monks wandering through the medieval countryside, a direct affront to St. Benedict's Rule, which dictates strict confinement to the monastery.

B. Ignoring the precept of poverty, which implies a complete renunciation of personal property, most medieval monks had possessions, ranging from costume jewelry to slaves, and varying amounts of money.

C. By tradition and St. Benedict's Rule, butcher's meat was forbidden to the monks except under certain conditions such as sickness or meals with guests, and eating was, at all times, to be in moderation; in actuality, however, monks were commonly satirized as gluttons, and meat was a standard part of their diet.

D. In disregard of the old Benedictine principle *ora et labora*, pray and work, virtually all monks had ceased any heavy manual labour by the medieval period and were primarily idle.

E. The sexual immorality of the monks, while not universal, nor as widespread as some of the other corruptions mentioned above, still existed to a significant degree; the fact that it existed at all is disturbing.

The Age of Faith, The Golden Age of Monasticism—epithets that are commonly applied to the European Middle Ages. They evoke in our minds a time of great Christian feeling, a time when the lives of most people revolved around the Church, and when a person of deep religious convictions naturally gravitated toward life in a monastic community, living piously in prayer and holy labor. Not so, for most inhabitants of medieval monasteries were not the devout and devoted individuals we often consider them to be; many were younger sons of nobles, with family property entailed away from them by primogeniture, who had no choice but to enter a monastery. Others were noble bastards, whose fathers wished them out of the way at a minimum expense, or criminals, for whom the tonsure was an alternative to prison. [1] Consequently, the pious and holy ideals of monastic life were very often set aside, the monks seeming to be rather members of a "rich bachelor fraternity"[2] than the spiritual and self-denying men they were supposed to be. In spite of the general irreligious atmosphere and the many infractions of the monastic Rules, the overall influence of the many abbeys and priories was positive, for they provided the opportunity to learn and study in a society where intellectual knowledge was usually secondary (especially among the lower classes) to physical prowess. The monks were also the medieval equivalent of a welfare and hostel system: they distributed alms and food to the needy and poor, and the monastery guest house was the temporary home of many travelers. The façade of the monasteries of Medieval Europe is that of a solid institution that benefited society. A closer look, however, reveals the many corruptions with which it was riddled. The gradual decline from the grand monastic tradition of St. Benedict's Rule, the first, and greatest, of the monastic Rules, and the secularization which accompanied it were typical of medieval monachism.

Despite this gradual deterioration of the monastic ideals during the Middle Ages, the Church in general, and the monasteries in particular, were the primary source of aid to the needy. According to monastic tradition, the monks offered charity in the form of food and alms to the poor, and hospitality by means of guest houses and meals to travelers, thus benefiting much of the population. In the medieval era society consisted primarily of two classes: the very rich and the very poor. During times of famine and distress the poor were often left completely desolate, and the monasteries were a place of refuge for them, providing a home and food. *The Chronicle of Evesham*, written in England shortly after the Conqueror, states that during one disaster "a vast multitude of men old and young, and of women with their little ones, came to Evesham in their distress, fleeing from famine, all these Aethilwild (the Abbot) supported as best he could."[3] But the monasteries were sources of relief not only during isolated times of distress, for almost every day of the year was a day of need to the very poor, and the monks serviced this need also. They distributed alms through a daily dole, and any extras from the monastic table were given to the poor. One famous Rule, the *Regularis Concordia* (the Regular Canons were one of the larger Orders in England during this period), stipulates that "accommodation and livelihood should be provided by each monastery for a certain number of the poor."[4] The other important charitable contribution the monks had to offer was that of their guest houses. All pilgrims, whether traveling relatively short distances or making long journeys, stayed at the monastic "hotels," and many other travelers did also because the only cost of accommodation was any contribution the guest might make to the monastic funds. In all, between 3–10% of the total monachal income was given out as charity in one form or another,[5] a substantial contribution when it is considered how rich many of these monasteries were.

Charity was not the only contribution medieval monachism had to make; the monasteries were also great centers for intellectual and cultural growth, for the monks were among the most educated people in the world, and they initiated a great many of the important advances in literature, architecture and music. Close examination of a list of important medieval books reveals the many famous monastic authors. Books such as *The Anglo-Saxon Chronicle* (a history of the Church ranging from its early years to 1154), the writings of the Venerable Bede (an early English monk who wrote on a variety of subjects), *The Chronicle of Jocelin de Brakelond* (a chronicle of St Edmund's Abbey at Bury, and particularly of its Abbot, Samson, as recorded by his chaplain Jocelin), and the famous book *Of the Imitation of Christ* by Thomas à Kempis, a German monk, are quite probably the most important books of the Middle Ages, for they show us the human side of medieval life and religion. But it is not only as actual authors that the monks exhibit their influence on literature. The hundreds of exquisite manuscripts of the Bible and other spiritual works, such as the prayer-book illustrated in Plate I,* all proclaim the skill of the monks working in the scriptorii. Also, the monastic libraries were the principal depositories of books during the medieval period,[6] often having as many as 300-600 books.[7] Another important artistic contribution of the monks was their interest in architecture. They built magnificent churches and chapterhouses, the most famous of which is probably Westminster Abbey (Plate II) or Canterbury Cathedral (Plate III) in England, with Mont St. Michel in Brittany not far behind (Plate IV). Their buildings were masterpieces of Gothic architecture, with tall spires reaching to the sky, glorious arched ceilings, and stained glass windows. It was in the choirs of these

---

* The author interleaved illustrations in the original essay.

spacious churches where another of the monachal contributions was appreciated: music. The medieval Church music was the very beginning of modern music. The Gregorian Chant, a single line of melody sung to the words of a prayer (the *Kyrie*, or the *Magnificat*, for example), was the first serious attempt at music since Roman times, but gradually composers began to write in harmony, generally for three voices. This Church music, well preserved because of the superior monastic scribes who were able to record the music for posterity, was the beginning of modern polyphony and is one of the most important monastic contributions of the Middle Ages,[8] along with the more tangible Church buildings and manuscripts. As can be seen, the monks in medieval times left us many bequests, not least among them these advances in literature, architecture, and music.

Despite the beneficial influence the monasteries had upon medieval society, they were not perfect. The feudal system was sweeping Europe at this time, and the monasteries were not left unaffected. As his monastery began to possess more and more land, the medieval abbot found himself to be increasingly estranged from the ordinary life of his abbey. As a feudal lord, and vassal, the abbot was expected to be present at his lord's court, often that of the King, which took him away from his cloister for long stretches of time.[9] The Rule of St. Benedict, the most influential of the medieval Rules, stipulates that although the abbot has almost unlimited power, and is the most important person in the abbey,[10] he is to live as an ordinary member of the community;[11] the only exceptions to this rule were that the abbot was allowed to sleep not in the common dormitory but in his own private room, and that he was allowed to dine not at the communal table of the refectory but instead with any guests the monastery might have. But, as time went by, many abbots bypassed these simple, practical exemptions from the Rule and, with the excuse of feudal duties, took advantage of them. The abbot's "room apart" gradually became a complete establishment consisting of his own hall, court, garden (Plate V—prior's establishment) and a chapel where he heard mass daily instead of reciting the office with the community. [12] His "baronial dignity" [13] often expressed itself in what one historian terms "palatial lodgings" [14] that often included great parks and country houses. Even Abbot Samson, the hero of Jocelin's *Chronicle*, spent a great deal of time away from the abbey at his manor at Melford, proclaiming that he preferred country life. [15] This secularization, which caused the abbots of a landed monastery to seem to be barons rather than anything resembling monks, was reflected in the qualities looked for in the choice of an abbot. By the "middle" of the Middle Ages, the first choice was no longer someone extraordinarily saintly and pious, but rather someone who possessed great business acumen. In the words of Sir Arthur Bryant:

> The age of monastic saints had passed; what was now admired in conventual circles was a dignified, shrewd man of the world who combined the conventional Christian virtues with a keen eye for his house's interests. [16]

In fact, many abbots were appointed by a lord or king, as opposed to having been elected by their monks, and were entirely unsuited for spiritual office. Abbot Roger is an example: after his appointment by the king to the position of abbot at Evesham Abbey in 1189, the power of his office went to his head, and he was eventually deposed as a petty tyrant, having starved the monks and committed other sins. [17] Even those chosen by their own communities were by the 12th century less pious than abbots had been in the early days of monasticism; Samson was generally acknowledged to be "more of an administrator than an ecclesiastic"[18] and at the seige of Windsor was, in the words of Jocelin, who admired him very greatly, "more remarkable there for his counsel than for his piety."[19] Samson was typical of his age: a skillful administrator as opposed to a pious saint, who enjoyed the privileges his office gave him and took full advantage of them.

The importance of the secularization of the abbots, and the far-reaching consequences it had, can be understood when one realizes the influence the character of an abbot had upon his monastery. Since the abbot was the very "pivot on which the life of the monastery turned,"[20] his character had a great effect on the monks; if he were a strong, spiritual man, the monastery would follow suit, but, conversely, if he were either weak, or highly secular, the monks could do (and did) as they pleased. According to St. Benedict's Rule, the abbot should be the very center of the monastic life and no major decisions could be made without his approval. He should also set an example for his monks "in deeds rather than words all that is good and holy."[21] When the abbot did set an example of goodness and holiness, as Abbot Samson of Bury St. Edmunds did, the monastery prospered. Despite the financial mess it had fallen into under the previous Abbot, Hugh, Samson pulled the monastery out of deep debt through his example of paying back debts, not borrowing any more money, and not spending more than necessary. Hugh had been old, and had grown weak, and thus had not kept track of his monks' business matters. A quotation from Jocelin's *Chronicle* says it very aptly:

> Abbot Hugh had by this time grown old . . . ; pious and kindly he was, but neither good nor provident in this world's business . . . in the external matters, things were going badly, for, since they were serving under a lord that was simple and growing

old, every man did as he wished, not as he ought. [22]

For the monks of St. Edmunds, doing as they wished seemed to indicate overspending the money allotted to them for their crafts, and subsequently going into debt. The sacristan alone had sealed £3,052 in debts under Abbot Hugh,[23] but when Samson became abbot, the debts were uncovered and paid back, and the culprit was deposed. Abbot Hugh himself had placed the Abbey into debt for over £2,300,[24] mostly to Jews, who charged interest, as opposed to Christians, who did not, setting a poor example for his monks, who, as it has been demonstrated, followed it. The principle that the abbot should hold "Christ's place"[25] in the monastery was sometimes followed; what was *always* true, however, was that when an abbot set an example, the monks followed it.

The monks *did* follow the abbatial example, with the result that the high ideals set forth in the monastic Rules were often rendered corrupt by not being followed word for word, and were sometimes abandoned almost entirely. Just how corrupt the monasteries were can be seen by examining several common infractions of the Rule, and seeing how extensive they were. One of the most common, and certainly among the most commented on by contemporaries was the frequent absence of the monks from their monasteries, sometimes on feudal business, but more often on trips for pleasure. Since they followed the secular example set by the abbots, it was a common sight to see monks wandering through the medieval countryside, a direct affront to St. Benedict's Rule, which dictates strict confinement to the monastery. All monastic sources point to cloisterization as something necessary for the good of the monastery: St. Benedict decrees it in his Rule,[26] and St. Jerome, in describing the "model monk" states that this monk is only capable of living in his cloister, and once outside it, dies "like a fish out of water."[27] Examples of St.

Jerome's model of monachal goodness were few and far between, and Chaucer, in the General Prologue of *The Canterbury Tales*, has the monk, out of his cloister for a pleasant spring pilgrimage to Canterbury, refute this monastic ideal:

> He did not rate that text at a plucked hen
> Which says that hunters are not holy men
> And that a monk uncloistered is a mere
> Fish out of water, flapping on the pier,
> That is to say, a monk out of his cloister.
> That was a text he held not worth an oyster.[28]

Although Chaucer was writing fiction, his writing is a comment on his society, and reflects the realities of the time, as does the very famous *Vision of Piers Plowman,* believed to have been written by William Langland in the 14th century, where the author laments:

> As now is Religioun a ryder, a rowmer bi stretes,
> A leder of love-dayes and a londe-buyer,
> A priker on a palfray fro manere to manere,
> An heep of houndes at his ers, as he a lorde were.[29]

These comments of the people (for Chaucer was not a cleric, and Langland is believed to have taken only minor orders) upon the state of monachism are very valuable, for they show that it is not only ourselves looking back who consider this aspect of monastic life corrupt. It is, however, also valuable to look back at statements of the monks themselves. In 1444, the English General Chapter of Benedictines imposed standard punishments for various offenses such as lying, or striking a fellow monk. Among them was the punishment of temporary conformity to the regulation of monastic confinement for periods ranging from three weeks to one year.[30] This decree is amusing when one considers that confinement to the cloister was supposed to be a permanent and integral part of the daily adherence to the Rule; obviously little attention was now paid to it. This example shows how wide-spread absence from the monasteries was, if even those in charge of monastic morals considered it usual, and did not try to curtail it, while inflicting punishments for other infractions.

Another corruption of monastic life was the absence of poverty among the monks. The "Three Substantials" of monachism were Poverty, Chastity, and Obedience, from which, supposedly, no monk could ever be released.[31] But ignoring this precept of poverty, which implies a complete renunciation of personal property, most medieval monks had possessions, ranging from costume jewelry to slaves, and varying amounts of money. Many flaunted their possessions openly: Chaucer's prioress—

> She wore a coral trinket on her arm,
> A set of beads, the gaudies tricked in green,
> Whence hung a golden brooch of brightest sheen
> On which there first was graven a crowned A,
> And lower, *Amor vincit omnia.*[32]

Even if one overlooks the *Amor vincit omnia* (love conquers all), her decoration is hardly monastic, and neither is that of her companion The Monk, of whom Chaucer says:

> He had a wrought gold cunningly fashioned pin;
> Into a lover's knot it seemed to pass.[33]

Such repeated observations of very unmonastic jewelry on monastics seem to underscore how commonplace such behavior was. Once again, a statement from a General Chapter inadvertently gives an insight on the frequency of unorthodox behavior—in this case, monks possessing slaves. The General Chapter of the Cistercians, a "reformed" monastic order, states:

> We decree, under pain of deposition and expulsion, that no person of this Order presume to purchase Saracen women as concubines to their Saracen slaves, for any cause whatsoever.[34]

Information that monks had personal slaves, and money to buy concubines for them is issued with no mention of shame. It thus appears that slaveholding was relatively commonplace and acceptable; only the purchase of concubines warranted punishment. The pocket-money the monks appear to have possessed came from various sources: some monks embezzled, like the sacristan at Bury St. Edmunds in 1185, who at his death was found to be in possession of a fortune.[35] Others accepted bribes, like Abbot Samson, for whom "ten marks, as it is said, 'did blind the eyes of the wise.'"[36] Possessions were widespread among monks; in some monasteries each monk had his own apartments[37] instead of the monks sharing a common dorter, and at Launceston, an English monastery of the Regular Canons, every canon had his own room, personal servant, dog, herb garden, and dovecote, as well as a cash allowance for trifles.[38] "Proprietary" monks, as they were termed in the Middle Ages,[39] were a very serious lesion in the body of the church and contributed greatly to her corruption.

> Which, I ask, is the graver transgression in the matter of flesh-eating? That of the Black monks [Benedictines], who eat it openly, or of the White monks [Cistercians], who (as it is said) often eat it secretly to repletion? For both have the same Benedictine Rule.[40]

This quotation from the 14th century canonist John of Oyton states plainly how widespread the problem of monastic gluttony and flesh-eating was. By tradition and St. Benedict's Rule, butcher's meat was forbidden to the monks except under certain conditions such as sickness or meals with guests,[41] and eating was, at all times, to be in moderation;[42] in actuality, however, monks were commonly satirized as gluttons, and meat was a standard part of their diet. By the High Middle Ages, the number of monks pretending to be sick, or merely eating at the infirmary, where they could get meat, had grown so great that by a papal decree, at any given time, one-half of the monks were allowed to eat meat in a place called the "misericord" just outside the infirmary.[43] Although in theory the monastic diet consisted of merely two cooked dishes, bread, fruit, and beer or wine[44] (not haute cuisine by any standards), the table of a well-off monastery was a byword for good dining.[45] As an example, the chronicler Abailard said:

> Every lean fellow, when he reacheth this stew pond of the cloister, soon waxeth so fat and well-liking that, seeing him again after a brief while, thou shalt scarce know him for what he was.[46]

The 12th century archdeacon and monastic critic Giraldus Cambrensis, Gerald of Wales, spoke a great deal about the gluttony of monks everywhere. In this passage he deplores the eating habits of the monks at Canterbury Cathedral because of the tendency of gluttony to corrupt the whole moral structure of the monastic system. It seems to sum up the problem of monastic gluttony quite well:

> This added heaven of gluttony proceeded forthwith to dissolve and corrupt the whole lump of pristine probity.[47]

As the feudal system took hold in medieval Europe, the monasteries grew increasingly rich, and as is the custom of people everywhere when they become wealthy, the monks gradually discontinued their manual toil. In disregard of the old Benedictine principle *ora et labora*, pray and work,[48] virtually all monks had ceased any heavy manual labor by the medieval period and were primarily idle. All hard work was done by servants, the number of which often equaled, and sometimes exceeded, the number of monks.[49] These servants did all manual work except writing, manuscript copying, and any craft work the monks might do.[50] The work in the fields (which St. Benedict specifically mentions as a blessing for all monks),[51] cleaning, cooking—all were done by hired servants, lay brothers, or serfs.[52] This was deplored by several contemporary chroniclers who felt that this basic laziness was harmful to the spiritual atmosphere of the monastery and contrary to St. Benedict's statement that "idleness is an enemy of the soul."[53] One of these monastic chroniclers, Abailard, said:

> We, who ought to live by the labour of our own hands (which alone as St. Benedict saith maketh us truly monks), do now follow after idleness, that enemy of the soul, and seek our livelihood from the labours of other men.[54]

This relatively general statement condemning the common idleness of the monks is expanded upon by Peter the Venerable of Cluny who, in lamenting the corrupt nature of his own very famous "reformed" monastery, said:

> Idleness, which our Father St. Benedict calleth the enemy of the soul, had gotten such a hold upon a great number of our inmates, and especially upon the so-called lay brethren [brothers not having

taken full orders; generally the ones who did the most manual work in a monastery] that, both within and without the cloister they either slept against the walls of the cloister or wasted the whole day, almost from sunrise to sunset—nay, almost into midnight, when they might do it with impunity—in vain, idle, and worse still, often-times in back biting talk.[55]

The continual sloth of these monks numbed both their bodies and their souls, defeating the purpose of the tenet of *ora et labora,* which was to stimulate the mind as well as the body by moderate labor,[56] and also to prevent instances such as the "backbiting talk" mentioned above.

The inactivity of the monks was reflected not only in immoral talk, but also in immoral actions.

In many monasteries they led a carnal life; for the brethren, having no spiritual delights, sought those of the flesh.[57]

This quotation from Humbert de Romans, a 12th-century chronicler, is a sad commentary on the moral state of medieval monastic life. The sexual immorality of the monks, while not universal, nor as wide-spread as some of the other corruptions mentioned above, still existed to a significant degree; the fact that unchastity existed at all is disturbing. At the time of the Dissolution of the Monasteries in England (1536) some 251 persons were charged with "incontinence" and 189 with sodomy.[58] These figures were somewhat exaggerated by the "visitors" to the monasteries, who were, after all, trying to find reasons to disband them, but nonetheless, the figures are quite large, even when exaggeration is taken into account. Other con-temporaries commented on the comparatively frequent unchastity of monks also; St. Odo of Cluny in 942 sadly declaimed that "the vow of chastity is only too commonly broken,"[59] and Giraldus Cambrensis relates the story of a knight making a pilgrimage to the shrine of St. James of Compostela in Spain who is told that "the monks of these parts keep their mistresses and lemans publically; . . . the Order is not so strict hereabouts."[60] The names of those rumored to have sinned is endless: well-known personages such as the Abbot of Bardney, [61] the Abbot of Peterborough [62] and Abbot Roger of Evesham[63] are notorious examples. The violation of this one of the Three Substantials (Poverty, Chastity, and Obedience) is more serious than the violations of the others, for Poverty and Obedience were rules for monks only, while Chastity is one of the ten commandments and is therefore supposed to be a rule for everyone. The fact that the monks did not observe even the rule of chastity indicates how much they were drawn to the secular example, which further shows how immoral the monasteries had become.

Were the Middle Ages really the "Golden Age of Monasticism"? They started well enough in 547 with the writing of St. Benedict's Rule, which has dictated the precepts and ideals of monastic life ever since, but they ended ingloriously when Henry VIII dissolved the monasteries in 1536. What about the intervening years? Was the promise of the Rule carried out, or was there a steady downward path to the Dissolution? In fact, there was neither, but instead something of a compromise. Although the institution of monasticism contributed greatly to medieval life through a distribution of charity and the atmosphere of learning and culture which surrounded it, the daily life of the individual monastery was often rendered corrupt by the frequent bypassing, both by the abbots and the monastic community in general, of the traditions and the way of life established by St. Benedict's Rule.

NOTES

[1] George Gordon Coulton, St. Bernard, His Predecessors and Successors, 1000-1200 A.D. (Cambridge: The University Press, 1923) 62, vol. I of Five Centuries of Religion.

[2] Sir Arthur Bryant, The Age of Chivalry (Garden City: Doubleday and Co. Inc., 1963) 350.

[3] David Knowles, The Monastic Order in England (Cambridge: The University Press, 1940) 484-485.

[4] Knowles 482.

[5] J. Thomas Kelly, Thorns on the Tudor Rose: Monks, Vagabonds and Sturdy Beggars (Jackson: University Press of Mississippi, 1977) 28.

[6] Knowles 523.

[7] Knowles 525.

[8] Beverly Taylor, "Renaissance Music," The Winsor School, Boston, Fall 1978.

[9] Lowrie John Daly, Benedictine Monasticism: Its Formation and Development Through the Twelfth Century (New York: Sheed and Ward, 1965) 216.

[10] E. C. Butler, Benedictine Monachism: Studies in Benedictine Life and Rule (London: Longmans, Green and Co., 1919) 187.

[11] Daly 215.

[12] Knowles 405-406.

[13] Coulton 46.

[14] Bryant 349.

[15] Jocelin de Brakelond, The Chronicle of Jocelin de

Brakelond, trans. Sir Ernest Clarke (London: Alexander Moring, The de le Mare Press, 1903) xxxviii.

[16] Bryant 350.

[17] Daly 224.

[18] de Brakelond xxxvii.

[19] de Brakelond 82.

[20] Butler 184.

[21] Benedict, The Rule of St. Benedict, trans. Cardinal Gasquet (London: Chatto & Windus, 1925) 10-11.

[22] Daly 231.

[23] de Brakelond 3-4.

[24] de Brakelond 5.

[25] Butler 184.

[26] Benedict 119.

[27] George Gordon Coulton, The Friars and the Dead Weight of Tradition, 1200-1400 A.D. (Cambridge: The University Press, 1927) 13, vol. 2 of Five Centuries of Religion.

[28] Geoffrey Chaucer, The Canterbury Tales, trans. Nevill Coghill (Baltimore: Penguin Books, 1952) 29.

[29] Coulton, The Friars 12.

[30] Coulton, The Friars 13-14.

[31] George Gordon Coulton, The Medieval Scene: An Informal Introduction to the Middle Ages (Cambridge: The University Press, 1930) 75.

[32] Chaucer 29.

[33] Chaucer 30.

[34] Coulton, St. Bernard 394.

[35] George Gordon Coulton, Getting and Spending (Cambridge: The University Press, 1936) 370, vol. 3 of Five Centuries of Religion.

[36] de Brakelond 200.

[37] Bryant 355.

[38] Bryant 355.

[39] Coulton, Getting and Spending 367.

[40] Coulton, St. Bernard 392.

[41] Daly 207.

[42] Benedict 73.

[43] Coulton, The Medieval Scene 19.

[44] Benedict 73-74.

[45] Bryant 351.

[46] Coulton, St. Bernard 266.

[47] Coulton, The Friars 95.

[48] Friedrich Heer, The Medieval World: Europe 1100-1350 (Cleveland: The World Publishing Co., 1961) 41.

[49] Daly 222.

[50] Coulton, The Friars 175.

[51] Benedict 85.

[52] Heer 41.

[53] Benedict 84.

54 Coulton, St. Bernard 266.

55 Coulton, St. Bernard 268.

56 Benedict 85.

57 Coulton, St. Bernard 524.

58 Kelly 8.

59 Coulton, St. Bernard 262.

60 Coulton, The Friars 95.

61 Giraldus Cambrensis, as qtd. in Coulton, The Friars 96.

62 Coulton, The Medieval Scene 84.

63 Giraldus Cambrensis, as qtd. in Will Durant, The Age of Faith (New York: Simon and Schuster, 1950) 786.

LIST OF ILLUSTRATIONS

(In the original paper the list of illustrations was placed after the contents. Each illustration was given a Plate number—e.g. Plate I, Plate II, etc.—and was credited according to standard citation forms.)

BIBLIOGRAPHY

Benedict. The Rule of St. Benedict. Trans. Cardinal
Gasquet. London: Chatto & Windus, 1925.

Bryant, Sir Arthur. The Age of Chivalry. Garden City:
Doubleday and Co. Inc., 1963.

Butler, E. C. Benedictine Monachism: Studies in
Benedictine Life and Rule. London: Longmans, Green
and Co., 1919.

Chaucer, Geoffrey. The Canterbury Tales. Trans. Nevill
Coghill. Baltimore: Penguin Books, 1952.

Coulton, George Gordon. The Friars and the Dead
Weight of Tradition, 1200- 1400 A.D. Cambridge: The
University Press, 1927. Vol. 2 of Five Centuries of
Religion.

- - - . Getting and Spending. Cambridge: The University
Press, 1936. Vol 3 of Five Centuries of Religion.

- - - . The Medieval Scene: An Informal Introduction to
the Middle Ages. Cambridge: The University Press,
1930.

- - - . St. Bernard, His Predecessors and Successors,
1000-1400 A.D. Cambridge: The University Press,
1927. Vol. I of Five Centuries of Religion.

Daly, Lowrie John. Benedictine Monasticism: Its
Formation and Development Through the Twelfth
Century. New York: Sheed and Ward, 1965.

de Brakelond, Jocelin. The Chronicle of Jocelin de

Brakelond. Trans. Sir Ernest Clarke. London: Alexander Moring, The de la Mare Press, 1903.

Dickinson, John Compton. Monastic Life in Medieval England. New York: Barnes and Noble, 1961.

Durant, Will. The Age of Faith. New York: Simon and Schuster, 1950.

Heer, Friedrich. The Medieval World: Europe 1100-1350. Trans. Janet Sondheimer. Cleveland: The World Publishing Co., 1961.

Kelly, J. Thomas. Thorns on the Tudor Rose: Monks, Vagabonds and Sturdy Beggars. Jackson: University Press of Mississippi, 1977.

Knowles, David. The Monastic Order in England: A History of Its Development from the Times of St. Dunstan to the Fourth Lateran Council, 943-1216. Cambridge: The University Press, 1940.

- - - . Saints and Scholars: Twenty-Five Medieval Portraits. Cambridge: TheUniversity Press, 1963.

Taylor, Beverly. "Renaissance Music." A lecture given at the Winsor School, Boston. Fall, 1978.

Index